Understanding
the
Cults

BOOKS BY JOSH MCDOWELL
Reasons Skeptics Should Consider Christianity
Prophecy: Fact or Fiction
More Than a Carpenter
Evidence That Demands a Verdict
Evidence Growth Guide: The Uniqueness of Christianity
More Evidence That Demands a Verdict
The Resurrection Factor
The Resurrection Factor Growth Guide
Answers to Tough Questions
Givers, Takers and Other Kinds of Lovers
Handbook of Today's Religions—Understanding the Cults
Handbook of Today's Religions—Understanding the Occult
Handbook of Today's Religions—Understanding
Non-Christian Religions

Josh McDowell & Don Stewart

◈ HANDBOOK OF ◈ TODAY'S RELIGIONS

Understanding the Cults

CAMPUS CRUSADE FOR CHRIST
Published by
HERE'S LIFE PUBLISHERS, INC.
San Bernardino, California 92402

HANDBOOK OF TODAY'S RELIGIONS
UNDERSTANDING THE CULTS
by Josh McDowell and Don Stewart

A Campus Crusade for Christ Book

Published by
HERE'S LIFE PUBLISHERS, INC.
P. O. Box 1576
San Bernardino, CA 92402

ISBN 0-86605-090-6
HLP Product No. 402826
Library of Congress Catalogue Card 81-81850
© Copyright 1982 by Campus Crusade for Christ, Inc.
All rights reserved.

Manufactured in the United States of America

FOR MORE INFORMATION, WRITE:

L. I. F. E. — P. O. Box A399, Sydney South 2000, Australia
Campus Crusade for Christ of Canada — Box 368, Abbottsford, B. C., V25 4N9, Canada
Campus Crusade for Christ — 103 Friar Street, Reading RGl IEP, Berkshire, England
Campus Crusade for Christ — 28 Westmoreland St., Dublin 2, Ireland
Lay Institute for Evangelism — P. O. Box 8786, Auckland 3, New Zealand
Life Ministry — P. O. Box / Bus 91015, Auckland Park 2006, Republic of So. Africa
Campus Crusade for Christ, Int'l. — Arrowhead Springs, San Bernardino, CA 92414, U.S.A.

"Beloved, believe not every spirit, but try the spirits whether they are of God, because many false prophets are gone out into the world" (1 John 4:1 KJV).

Table of Contents

Why This Book?

Over the years the authors have had many requests to write a book on the various alternatives to Christianity — the cults, non-Christian religions, secular religions, and the occult. This volume is the first in a series of works dealing with these subjects.

Frequently we are challenged by people of other religious beliefs when we affirm the uniqueness and finality of the Christian faith. They argue that Christianity is compatible with other religions and cults and that we should not stress the uniqueness of Jesus Christ as being the only way a person can know the true and living God. This series demonstrates that Christianity is *not* compatible with cults, non-Christian religions, secular religions, or the occult.

It should also be pointed out that it is not Christianity that has attacked the cults, but rather, the cults have attacked Christianity. The result is that orthodox Christianity has had to go on the defensive, presenting its truth to combat the deviations the cults wish to perpetrate as historic Christian doctrine.

The Scope of Our Study

This series is intended to be a general reference work for those who are interested in knowing what various groups believe and why those beliefs are not compatible with biblical Christianity. It is not intended to be an exhaustive treatise on any one group or a comprehensive guide to all alternatives to Christianity. Rather, we have confined ourselves to deal with specific groups with which we have had the most contact. However, because we haven't dealt with a particular group doesn't mean we advocate its beliefs.

In addition, it has been necessary for us to limit ourselves to evaluating the central beliefs of each chosen group, spending little time dealing with its history, organization, methods, or secondary beliefs, unless specifically related to their doctrines in a fashion that thus warrants consideration.

Our desire is for this work to serve as a useful reference and springboard for further study. We have also prepared an extensive annotated bibliography to give the reader further help if he wishes to know more about any one group. For someone who desires a book on sharing Christ with those in the cults, we highly recommend *Answers to the Cultist at Your Door* by Robert and Gretchen Passantino, Harvest House Publishers, 1981.

The Proper Attitude

We live in a society where a person has the freedom to follow the religious belief of his or her choice. We have no quarrel with this. However, when individuals or groups publicly claim they are now God's true work here upon the earth and orthodox Christianity, which has existed throughout the centuries, is now wrong, we feel we must answer such challenges. They have the freedom to say it, but as Christians we have the responsibility to answer them.

The Bible commands us to "be ready always to give an answer to every man that asketh you a reason of the hope that is in you with meekness and fear" (1 Peter 3:15 KJV). This work is that answer to those who have attacked historic Christianity and placed their own beliefs above it. We are not attacking these groups; we are merely answering their accusations. An example of the type of accusations we are answering can be found in the writings of The Church of Jesus Christ of the Latter-day Saints, better known as the Mormons.

> Every intelligent person under the heavens that does not, when informed, acknowledge that Joseph Smith, Jr., is a prophet of God, is in darkness and is opposed to us and to Jesus and His kingdom on the earth (*Journal of Discourses* 8:223).
>
> What does the Christian world know about God? Nothing;...Why, so far as the things of God are concerned, they are the veriest fools; they know neither God nor the things of God (*Journal of Discourses* 13:225).

We cannot allow these types of accusations to pass. They must be answered. However, in answering the charges made by the cults and other non-Christian groups, we desire to do so without resorting to name-calling or sarcasm. It is possible to disagree with a person's beliefs and yet love the person holding those beliefs. What we oppose is the teachings of these groups, not the people in the groups nor their right to believe whatever they want. We speak out because the Bible commands us to "earnestly contend for the faith which has been once and for all delivered" (Jude 3).

Finally, the Apostle Paul has exhorted us to "prove all things; hold fast that which is good" (1 Thessalonians 5:21 KJV). That is what this series is all about.

CHAPTER ONE

What Is a Cult?

A cult is a perversion, a distortion of biblical Christianity and as such, rejects the historic teachings of the Christian church. The Apostle Paul warned there would be false Christs and a false gospel that would attempt to deceive the true church and the world.

> For if one comes and preaches another Jesus whom we have not preached, or you receive a different spirit which you have not received, or a different gospel which you have not accepted, you bear this beautifully...for such men are false apostles, deceitful workers, disguising themselves as apostles of Christ and no wonder for even Satan disguises himself as an angel of light. Therefore it is not surprising if his servants also disguise themselves as servants of righteousness; whose end shall be according to their deeds (2 Corinthians 11: 13-15 NASB).

Walter Martin gives us a good definition of a cult when he says:

> A cult, then, is a group of people polarized around someone's interpretation of the Bible and is characterized by major deviations from orthodox Christianity relative to the cardinal doctrines of the Christian faith, particularly the fact that God became man in Jesus Christ (Walter Martin, *The Rise of the Cults*, p. 12).

Why Do Cults Prosper?

We live in a day in which the cults show rapid growth. For example:

> The Mormon Church has grown from 30 members in 1830 to more than 4,000,000 as of April, 1978, and its growth rate is a religious phenomenon. In 1900 the church numbered 268,331; in 1910, 393,437; in 1920, 526,032; in 1930, 672,488; in 1940, 862,664; in 1950, 1,111,314; in 1960, 1,693,180; in 1962, 1,965,786; in 1964, over 2,000,000 members, and in 1976 their projection for the year 2000 was for more than 8,000,000 members (Walter Martin, *The Maze of Mormonism*, p. 16).

We believe there are several basic reasons people join cults and why they prosper.

The Cults Provide Answers

A major reason the cults are flourishing is that in an unsure world they provide authoritative answers to man's basic questions: *Who am I? Why am I here? Where am I going?*

Max Gunther, the writer, describes the plight of a young woman, common to many in our generation. "I thought I wanted to become a nurse but I wasn't sure. I thought Christianity meant a lot to me but I wasn't sure of that either. I guess I was kind of desperately looking for somebody who had firm yes-and-no answers, somebody who was sure about things and could make me sure" (*Today's Health*, February, 1976, p. 16).

Unfortunately, this young lady eventually joined a cult which willingly supplied her with answers. She put it this way, "I kept going back and asking them questions and they always knew the answers—I mean, really knew them." Thus the cults offer certainty and easy answers to those who are unsatisfied with the present state of their lives.

The Cults Meet Human Needs

Cults also flourish because they appeal to man's basic human need. All of us need to be loved, to feel needed, to sense our lives have direction and meaning. Individuals who experience an identity crisis or have emotional problems are particularly susceptible to cults. During such difficult moments, many cults give the unsuspecting a feeling of acceptance and direction.

Furthermore, within all of us there is a basic desire to know and serve God. The cults take advantage of this and offer ready-made, but ultimately unsatisfying, solutions. Most cults tell their followers what to believe, how to behave and what to think, and emphasize dependence upon the group or leader for their emotional stability. The Passantinos give an example of this:

> A person does not usually join a cult because he has done an exhaustive analysis of world religions and has decided that a particular cult presents the best theology available. Instead, a person usually joins a cult because he has problems that he is having trouble solving, and the cult promises to solve these problems. Often these problems are emotional.
>
> We talked to a young man who had just left the army, hadn't been discharged a week, and had already joined the Children of God (the Family of Love) and had given them 100 dollars. He said that he was lonely, wanted to serve God, and didn't know where to go or what to do. The Family of Love seized on his loneliness, smothered him with love and attention, and almost secured his permanent allegiance.
>
> Fortunately his mother called us and we talked to him, and within an hour he saw how wrong the cult was and decided not to join. We urged him to join a good small Bible study and to become involved in a strong church. Without a good Christian foundation and close relationships with other Christians, he would still be a candidate for the cults (Robert and Gretchen Passantino, *Answers to the Cultist at Your Door*, Harvest House, Eugene, Oregon, 1981, pp. 22, 23).

The Cults Make a Favorable Impression

The cults prosper because Christians have sometimes failed to be a vital influence in the world. Pierre Berton astutely noted:

> The virus that has been weakening the church for more than a generation is not the virus of anti-religious passion but the very lack of it...The Church to its opponents has become as a straw man, scarcely worth a bullet...Most ministers are scarcely distinguishable by their words, opinions, actions, or way of life from the nominal Christians and non-Christians

who form the whole of the community (Pierre Berton, *The Comfortable Pew*, Philadelphia: J. B. Lippincott, 1965, pp. 15-16).

If the church fails to carefully and seriously provide spiritual warmth and a true exposition of the Word of God, those with spiritual needs will find other avenues of fulfillment. Many cults prey on ignorance, and try to impress the uninformed with pseudo-scholarship.

An example is The Way International's leader, Victor Paul Wierwille, who quotes profusely from Hebrew and Greek sources in an attempt to give the impression of scholarship.

Representatives of Jehovah's Witnesses who go door to door give a similar impression of great learning. To combat this, the believer must know what he believes and why he believes it and thus be able to expose the cult's teachings.

Many people involved in the cults were raised in Christian churches but were untaught in basic Christian doctrine, making them prey for the cultists. Chris Elkins, a former Unification Church "Moonie" member, points this out:

> In most cults, a majority of the members left a mainline, denominational church. Perhaps in the church's attempt to explain why its members are leaving and joining cults, brainwashing is seen as an easy out.
>
> My contention is that brainwashing is really not the issue. In most cases we would be hard-pressed to isolate any element in the methodology of a cult that is not present in some form in mainstream churches. For Christians, the main issue with cults should be theology.
>
> Many of us accepted Christ at an early age. We had a child's understanding of Jesus, the Bible and salvation.
>
> That is okay for children and new Christians. But many of us older Christians are still babies spiritually. We have not learned to feed ourselves, much less anyone else (*Christian Life*, August 1980).

CHAPTER TWO

The Characteristics of Cults

Extensive travel throughout the United States and abroad, has made us aware of certain features that characterize the cults. These include:

New Truth

Many cults promote the false idea that God has revealed something special to them. This is usually truth that has never before been revealed and supersedes and contradicts all previous revelations. Sun Myung Moon's claim is that the mission of Christ was left unfinished and the world is now ready for the completion of Christ's work on earth.

The Unification Church teaches that the Rev. Moon is bringing truth previously unrevealed. Moon has said, "We are the only people who truly understand the heart of Jesus, the anguish of Jesus, and the hope of Jesus" (Rev. Moon, *The Way of the World*, Holy Spirit Ass'n for the Unification of World Christianity, Vol. VIII, No. 4, April, 1976).

The Mormon Church teaches that Christianity was in apostasy for some 18 centuries until God revealed new "truth" to Joseph Smith, Jr., restoring the true gospel that had been lost. Today the Mormon church has its living prophets who receive divine revelation from God, continually bringing new "truth" to the world.

These and other cults justify their existence by claiming they have something more than just the Bible and its "inadequate message."

The cults have no objective, independent way to test their teachings and practices. It's almost as though they feel just a firm assertion of their own exclusivity is sufficient proof of their anointing by God. However, as members of the universal Christian church, we can and should test all of our teachings and practices objectively and independently by God's infallible Word, the Bible, and history.

New Interpretations of Scripture

Some cults make no claim to new truth or extra-biblical revelation, but believe they alone have the key to interpreting the mysteries in the Bible. The Scriptures are their only acknowledged source of authority, but they are interpreted unreasonably and in a way different from that of orthodox Christianity. They testify that the historic beliefs and interpretations of Scripture are based upon a misunderstanding of the Bible or were pagan in origin. An example of this is found in the writings of Herbert W. Armstrong:

> ...I found that the popular church teachings and practices were not based on the Bible. They had originated...in paganism. The amazing, unbelievable TRUTH was, the sources of these popular beliefs and practices of professing Christianity was quite largely, paganism and human reasoning and custom, not the Bible! (Herbert W. Armstrong, *The Autobiography of Herbert W. Armstrong*, Pasadena: Ambassador College Press, 1967, p. 298, 294).

The Bible is then reinterpreted, usually out of context, to justify the peculiar doctrines of the cult. Without an objective and reasonable way to understand what the Bible teaches, the cult member is at the mercy of the theological whims of the cult leader.

A Non-biblical Source of Authority

Some cults have sacred writings or a source of authority that supersedes the Bible. The Mormon Church says, "We believe the Bible to be the Word of God in so far as it is translated correctly..." (*Articles of Faith of the Church of Jesus Christ of Latter-day Saints*, Article 8). Although this sounds like the Mormons trust the Bible, they, in fact,

believe it has been changed and corrupted. Listen to what
the Mormon apostle Talmage has said:

> There will be, there can be no absolutely reliable translation
> of these or other Scriptures unless it is effected through the
> gift of translation, as one of the endowments of the Holy
> Ghost...Let the Bible then be read reverently and with
> prayerful care, the reader ever seeking the light of the Spirit
> that he may discern between the truth and the errors of men
> (James E. Talmage, *The Articles of Faith*, Salt Lake City:
> Deseret News Press, 1968, p. 237).

Such a statement opens the door for their additional
sacred books, i.e., *The Book of Mormon, The Pearl of
Great Price* and *Doctrines and Covenants*, as greater
authoritative sources. Thus, the Bible is *not* truly their
final source of authority.

In Christian Science, the Bible is characterized as being
mistaken and corrupt and inferior to the writings of Mary
Baker Eddy.

The Unification Church believes the Bible to be in-
complete, while Rev. Moon's *Divine Principle* is the true
authoritative source.

Other groups such as The Way International and the
Worldwide Church of God claim the Bible to be their final
authority when in actuality their authority is the Bible as
interpreted by the cult leader. Regardless of whether the
Bible is superseded by other works or reinterpreted by a
cult leader, a sure mark of a cult is that the final authority
on spiritual matters rests on something other than the
plain teaching of Holy Scripture.

Another Jesus

One characteristic that is found in all cults is false
teaching about the person of Jesus Christ in the light of
historical biblical Christianity. The Apostle Paul warned
about following after "another Jesus" (2 Corinthians 11:4)
who is not the same Jesus who is revealed in Scripture.
The "Jesus" of the cults is always someone less than the
Bible's eternal God who became flesh, lived here on earth,
and died for our sins.

The Bible makes it clear that Jesus was God in human
flesh, second person of the Holy Trinity, who lived a
sinless life on earth and died as a sacrifice for the sins of

the world. Three days after His crucifixion, Jesus rose bodily from the dead. Fifty days afterward He ascended into heaven, where He now sits at the right hand of the Father, interceding on behalf of believers. He will, one day, return bodily to planet earth and judge the living and the dead while setting up His eternal Kingdom.

The Jesus of the cults is not the Jesus of the Bible.

According to the theology of the Jehovah's Witnesses, Jesus did not exist as God from all eternity but was rather the first creation of Jehovah God. Before coming to earth, He was Michael the Archangel, the head of all the angels. He is not God.

The Mormon Church does not accept the unique deity of Jesus Christ. He is, to them, one of many gods, the "first-born spirit child," spiritually conceived by a sexual union between the heavenly Father and a heavenly mother. He was also the spirit-brother of Lucifer in His preexistent state. His incarnation was accomplished by the physical union of the heavenly Father and the human Mary.

No matter what the particular beliefs of any cult may be, the one common denominator they all possess is a denial of the biblical teaching on the deity of Jesus Christ.

Rejection of Orthodox Christianity

Characteristic of many cultic groups is a frontal attack on orthodox Christianity. They argue that the church has departed from the true faith. Helena P. Blavatsky, founder of Theosophy, had this to say of orthodox Christianity:

> The name has been used in a manner so intolerant and dogmatic, especially in our day, that Christianity is now the religion of arrogance, par excellence, a stepping-stone for ambition, a sinecure for wealth, shame, and power; a convenient screen for hypocrisy (H. P. Blavatsky, *Studies in Occultism*, Theosophical University Press, n.d., p. 138).

Joseph Smith, Jr., the founder of Mormonism, said he was given this assessment of the Christian Church when he inquired of the Lord as to which church to join:

> ...I was answered that I must join none of them, for they were all wrong; and the personage who addressed me said that all their creeds were an abomination in His sight; that

those professors were all corrupt; that "they draw near to Me with their lips, but their hearts are far from Me, they teach for doctrines the commandments of men, having a form of godliness, but they deny the power thereof" (Joseph Smith, Jr., *The Pearl of Great Price*, 2:18-19).

Double-Talk

A feature of some cultic groups is that they say one thing publicly but internally believe something totally different. Many organizations call themselves Christians when in fact they deny the fundamentals of the faith.

The Mormon Church is an example of this kind of double-talk. The first article of faith in the Church of Jesus Christ of Latter-day Saints reads, "We believe...in His Son, Jesus Christ." This gives the impression Mormons are Christians since they believe in Jesus Christ. However, when we understand the semantics of what they mean by Jesus Christ, we discover they are far removed from orthodox Christianity. Nevertheless, the impression the Mormon Church gives from their advertising is that they are another denomination or sect of Christianity. One, therefore, must be on the alert for organizations that advertise themselves as "Christians" but whose internal teachings disagree with Scripture.

Non-biblical Teaching on the Nature of God (Trinity)

Another characteristic of all non-Christian cults is either an inadequate view or outright denial of the Holy Trinity. The biblical doctrine of the Trinity, one God in three Persons, is usually attacked as being pagan or satanic in origin.

The Jehovah's Witnesses are an example of this. They say, "There is no authority in the Word of God for the doctrine of the trinity of the Godhead" (Charles Russell, *Studies in the Scriptures*, V, Brooklyn: International Bible Students, 1912, p. 54). "The plain truth is that this is another of Satan's attempts to keep the God-fearing person from learning the truth of Jehovah and His Son Christ Jesus" (*Let God Be True*, Brooklyn: Watchtower Bible and Tract Society, 1946, p. 93).

The Way International takes a similar position. "Long before the founding of Christianity, the idea of a triune god or a god-in-three-persons was a common belief in ancient religions. Although many of these religions had 'many minor deities, they distinctly acknowledged that there was one supreme god who consisted of three persons or essences. The Babylonians used an equilateral triangle to represent this three-in-one god, now the symbol of the modern three-in-one believers" (*Jesus Christ Is Not God*, Victor Paul Wierville, New Knoxville, Ohio: American Christian Press, 1975, p. 11).

Cults, therefore, are marked by their deviation on the doctrine of the Trinity and the nature of God.

Changing Theology

Cult doctrines are continually in a state of flux and have no sure foundation on which to anchor their hope. Adherents of a particular cult will learn a doctrine only to find that doctrine later changed or contradicted by further revelation. Most cults will deny this, with the possible exception of the Unification Church. Recently they admitted their theology was in a state of flux.

The Jehovah's Witnesses, for example, used to believe vaccinations were sinful. Anyone who allowed himself to be vaccinated would lose his good standing in the organization. Today this is no longer taught.

Christianity Today, in an article interviewing William Cetnar (a former high official in the Jehovah's Witnesses), says:

> The controversial ban on receiving blood transfusions will probably be lifted after Franz's death, [Frederick Franz, 87, is the president of the Jehovah's Witnesses] Cetnar thinks.
>
> A new date for the end of the world (JWs have previously predicted Christ's return seven times) is likely to be announced, possibly 1988.
>
> By sheer mathematical necessity, some change will have to be made in the JW doctrine that Christ will return before an elect 144,000 Witnesses have died. The 144,000 places were filled by those living in 1914 and few remain alive today. But Christ is supposed to return before the entire generation has died (*Christianity Today*, Nov. 20, 1981, p. 70).

The Mormon Church is equally guilty of changing doctrine. The most famous is its belief and practice, later prohibited, of polygamy.

Strong Leadership

Cults are usually characterized by central leader figures who consider themselves messengers of God with unique access to the Almighty. Since the leader has such a special relationship with God, he can dictate the theology and behavior of the cult. Consequently, he exercises enormous influence over the group. This is true, for example, in the Unification Church, The Way International and the Worldwide Church of God.

This strong leadership leads the cult follower into total dependence upon the cult for belief, behavior and lifestyle. When this falls into the hands of a particularly corrupt leader, the results can be tragic, as with Jim Jones and the People's Temple tragedy. The more dramatic the claims of a cult leader, the more the possibility of a tragic conclusion.

Salvation by Works

One teaching that is totally absent from all the cults is the gospel of the grace of God. No one is taught in the cults that he can be saved from eternal damnation by simply placing his faith in Jesus Christ. It is always belief in Jesus Christ and "do this" or "follow that." All cults attach something to the doctrine of salvation by grace through faith. It might be baptism, obedience to the laws and ordinances of the gospel, or something else, but it is never taught that faith in Christ alone will save anyone.

Herbert W. Armstrong, founder and leader of the Worldwide Church of God, exemplifies this:

> Salvation, then, is a process! But how the God of this world would blind your eyes to that! He tries to deceive you into thinking all there is to it is just "accepting Christ" with "no works" — and presto-chango, you are pronounced "saved." But the Bible reveals that none is yet saved (Herbert W. Armstrong, *Why Were You Born?* p.11).

False Prophecy

Another feature of the cults is they often promulgate false prophecy. Cult leaders, who believe they have been divinely called by God, have made bold predictions of future events, supposedly revealed by the inspiration of God. Unfortunately, for the cult leaders, these predictions of future events do not come to pass. The one who prophesied is exposed as a false prophet.

Writing in 1967, Herbert W. Armstrong, (leader of the Worldwide Church of God), said, "Now other prophecies reveal we are to soon have (probably in about four years) such drought and famine, that disease epidemics will follow, taking millions of lives...Well, we have been getting foretastes of them! That condition is coming! And I do not mean in 400 years—nor in 40 years—but in the very next four or five!" (Herbert W. Armstrong, *The United States and British Commonwealth in Prophecy.* Pasadena: Ambassador College Press, 1967, p. 184).

The Jehovah's Witnesses have a well-established record of making false prophecies. This pattern was established by their founder and first president, Charles T. Russell, who conclusively prophesied the end of the world for 1914. Judge for yourself (1 John 4:1).

The Founder Speaks

1. "ALL PRESENT GOVERNMENTS WILL BE OVER-THROWN AND DISSOLVED" IN 1914.—*The Time Is At Hand,* pp. 98-99 (1889)

2. 1914—"THE FARTHEST LIMIT OF THE RULE OF IMPERFECT MAN."—*The Time Is At Hand,* p. 77 (1906 ed)*

3. "THE RE-ESTABLISHMENT OF ISRAEL IN THE LAND OF PALESTINE."—*Thy Kingdom Come,* p. 244, EARTHLY JERUSALEM TO BE RESTORED TO DIVINE FAVOR. —*The Time Is At Hand,* p.77

4. "THE FULL ESTABLISHMENT OF THE KINGDOM OF GOD *IN THE EARTH* AT A.D. 1914."—*Thy Kingdom Come,* p. 126 (1891)* "ON THE RUINS OF PRESENT INSTITUTIONS."—*The Time Is At Hand,* p. 77 (1912 ed)*

5. CHRIST WAS SPIRITUALLY PRESENT IN 1874. —*Thy Kingdom Come,* pp. 127-129, "AND WILL BE PRESENT AS EARTH'S NEW RULER" IN 1914.—*The Time Is At Hand,* p. 77

6. "BEFORE THE END OF A.D. 1914, THE LAST MEMBER OF THE 'BODY OF CHRIST' WILL BE

GLORIFIED WITH THE HEAD." – *The Time Is At Hand*, p. 77, (1906 ed)*

* The Watchtower Society in later editions made changes in what Russell stated here in an attempt to cover up his erroneous predictions.

Conclusion

While not every group that possesses these characteristics can be labeled a cult, beware of a group that embraces some of these features. The sure mark of a cult is what it does with the person of Jesus Christ. All cults ultimately deny the fact that Jesus Christ is God the Son, second Person of the Holy Trinity, and mankind's only hope.

CHAPTER THREE

The Beliefs of Orthodox Christianity

F or the last two thousand years, the Christian Church has held certain beliefs to be vital to one's faith. While there is some doctrinal disagreement within the three branches of Christendom—Roman Catholic, Eastern Orthodox and Protestant—there is a general agreement among them as to the essentials of the faith. Whatever disagreement the church may have among its branches, it is insignificant compared to the heretical non-Christian beliefs of the cults. We offer this section as a yardstick to compare the errant beliefs of the cults.

The Doctrine of Authority

When it comes to the matter of final authority there is agreement among the major branches of Christianity with regard to the divine inspiration of the Old and New Testaments. However, the Roman Catholic and Eastern Orthodox branches of the church go somewhat beyond the Bible as to their source of authority.

Roman Catholic   The historic Roman Catholic Church accepts the 66 books of the Old and New Testaments as the inspired Word of God. They also accept the Apocrypha as being inspired of God. Further, they consider church tradition just as authoritative as the Scriptures. (In a previous work, we have dealt with reasons why we do not accept the Apocrypha as sacred Scripture—*Answers*, Here's Life Publishers, 1980, pp. 36-38.)

Eastern Orthodox The historic Eastern Orthodox church also accepts the 66 books of the Old and New Testaments as God's inspired revelation. To this they add their church tradition as equally authoritative.

Protestant The historic Protestant church holds that Scripture alone is the final authority on all matters of faith and practice. The Lutheran formula of Concord put it this way: "We believe, confess, and teach that the only rule and norm, according to which all dogmas and doctrines ought to be esteemed and judged, is no other whatever than the prophetic and apostolic writings both of the Old and of the New Testaments."

Scripture itself testifies that it is complete in what it reveals and the standard and final authority on all matters of doctrine, faith and practice. "All Scripture is inspired by God and profitable for teaching, for reproof, for correction, for training in righteousness" (2 Timothy 3:16 NASB).

"But know this first of all, that no prophecy of Scripture is a matter of one's own interpretation, for no prophecy was ever made by an act of human will. But men moved by the Holy Spirit spoke from God" (2 Peter 1:20, 21 NASB).

"You shall not add to the word which I am commanding you, nor take away from it, that you may keep the commandments of the Lord your God which I command you" (Deuteronomy 4:2 NASB).

"I testify to everyone who hears the words of the prophecy of this book: if anyone adds to them, God shall add to him the plagues which are written in this book; and if anyone takes away from the words of the book of this prophecy, God shall take away his part from the tree of life and from the holy city, which are written in this book" (Revelation 22:18, 19 NASB).

The Doctrine of God

The Doctrine of God is the same in all three branches of Christianity. The Westminster Shorter Catechism (Question 6) reads, "There are three persons in the Godhead: the Father, the Son, and the Holy Ghost; and these three are one God, the same in substance, equal in power and glory."

The Athanasian Creed elaborates on the doctrine of the Trinity:

...we worship one God in Trinity, and Trinity in Unity; Neither confounding the Persons, nor dividing the Substance [Essence]. For there is one Person of the Father, another of the Son, and another of the Holy Ghost. But the Godhead of the Father, of the Son, and of the Holy Ghost is all one, the Glory equal, the Majesty co-eternal. Such as the Father is, such is the Son, and such is the Holy Ghost. The Father uncreate, the Son uncreate, and the Holy Ghost uncreate... The Father eternal, the Son eternal, and the Holy Ghost eternal. And yet they are not three eternals, but one eternal... So the Father is God, the Son is God, and the Holy Ghost is God. And yet they are not three Gods, but one God... the Unity in Trinity and the Trinity in Unity is to be worshipped.

In a previous work, *Answers to Tough Questions*, (Here's Life Publishers, 1980), we explained in a simple way the biblical doctrine of the Trinity. We are reprinting it here as an attempt to clarify what Orthodox Christianity believes regarding the nature of God.

One of the most misunderstood ideas in the Bible concerns the teaching about the Trinity. Although Christians say that they believe in one God, they are constantly accused of polytheism (worshipping at least three gods).

The Scriptures do *not* teach that there are three Gods; neither do they teach that God wears three different masks while acting out the drama of history. What the Bible does teach is stated in the doctrine of the Trinity as: there is *one* God who has revealed Himself in three persons, the Father, the Son and the Holy Spirit, and these three persons are the one God.

Although this is difficult to comprehend, it is nevertheless what the Bible tells us, and is the closest the finite mind can come to explaining the infinite mystery of the infinite God, when considering the biblical statements about God's being.

The Bible teaches that there is one God and only one God: "Hear, O Israel! The Lord is our God, the Lord is one!" (Deuteronomy 6:4 NASB). "There is one God" (1 Timothy 2:5 KJV). "Thus says the Lord, the King of Israel and his Redeemer, the Lord of hosts: 'I am the first and I am the last, and there is no God besides Me' " (Isaiah 44:6 NASB).

However, even though God is one in His essential being or nature, He is also three persons. "Let us make man in our image" (Genesis 1:26 KJV). "God said, Behold, the man has become like one of us" (Genesis 3:22 RSV).

God's plural nature is alluded to here, for He could not be talking to angels in these instances, because angels could not and did not help God create. The Bible teaches that Jesus Christ, not the angels, created all things (John 1:3; Colossians 1:15; Hebrews 1:2).

In addition to speaking of God as one, and alluding to a plurality of God's being, the Scriptures are quite specific as to naming God in terms of three persons. There is a person whom the Bible calls the Father, and the Father is designated as God the Father (Galatians 1:1).

The Bible talks about a person named Jesus, or the Son, or the Word, also called God. "The Word was God..." (John 1:1 KJV). Jesus was "also calling God His own Father, making Himself equal with God" (John 5:18 NASB).

There is a third person mentioned in the Scriptures called the Holy Spirit, and this person—different from the Father and the Son—is also called God ("Ananias, why has Satan filled your heart to lie to the Holy Spirit?... You have not lied to men, but to God," Acts 5:3,4 RSV).

The facts of the biblical teaching are these: There is one God. This one God has a plural nature. This one God is called the Father, the Son, the Holy Spirit, all distinct personalities, all designated God. We are therefore led to the conclusion that the Father, Son and Holy Spirit are one God, the doctrine of the Trinity.

Dr. John Warwick Montgomery offers this analogy to help us understand this doctrine better:

"The doctrine of the Trinity is not 'irrational'; what *is* irrational is to suppress the biblical evidence for Trinity in favor of unity, or the evidence for unity in favor of Trinity.

"Our data must take precedence over our models—or, stating it better, our models must sensitively reflect the full range of data.

"A close analogy to the theologian's procedure here lies in the work of the theoretical physicist: Subatomic light entities are found, on examination, to possess wave properties (W), particle properties (P), and quantum properties (h).

"Though these characteristics are in many respects incompatible (particles don't diffract, while waves do, etc.), physicists 'explain' or 'model' an electron as PWh. They have to do this in order to give proper weight to all the relevant data.

"Likewise the theologian who speaks of God as 'three in one.' Neither the scientist nor the theologian expects you to get a 'picture' by way of his model; the purpose of the model is to help you take into account *all* of the facts, instead of perverting reality through super-imposing an apparent 'consistency' on it.

"The choice is clear: either the Trinity or a 'God' who is only a pale imitation of the Lord of biblical and confessional Christianity" (*How Do We Know There is a God*, pp. 14, 15).

The Person of Jesus Christ

Two thousand years ago, Jesus asked His disciples the ultimate question: "Who do you say that I am?" (Matthew 16:15). Central to the Christian faith is the identity of its founder, Jesus Christ, and it is of monumental importance to have a proper view of who He is.

Jesus Was Human

The Christian Church has always affirmed that, although He was supernaturally conceived by the Holy Spirit, God in human flesh, Jesus Christ was also fully man. The teaching of the Scriptures is clear with regard to His humanity.

- He grew intellectually and physically.
  "Jesus kept increasing in wisdom and stature, and in favor with God and man" (Luke 2:52 KJV).

- He desired food.
  "And after He had fasted forty days and forty nights, He then became hungry" (Matthew 4:2 NASB).

- He became tired.
  "...Jesus therefore, being wearied from his journey..." (John 4:6 NASB).

- He needed sleep.
  "And behold, there arose a great storm in the sea, so that the boat was covered with the waves; but He Himself was asleep" (Matthew 8:24 NASB).

- He cried.
  "Jesus wept" (John 11:35).

- He died.
  "...but coming to Jesus, when they saw He was already dead, they did not break His legs." (John 11:33 NASB).

Therefore, it is made plain by Scripture that Jesus was genuinely human. He possessed all the attributes of humanity.

Jesus Was God

Jesus of Nazareth was a man but He was more than just a man. He was God in human flesh. While the Scriptures clearly teach He was a man, they likewise make it clear that he was God.

Jesus Made Divine Claims

There are many references by Jesus and His disciples concerning who He was.

- "In the beginning was the Word and the Word was with God and the Word was God" (John 1:1).
- "Jesus said to him,...He who has seen me has seen the Father" (John 14:9).
- "For this cause therefore the Jews were seeking all the more to kill Him, because He not only was breaking the Sabbath, but also was calling God His own Father, making Himself equal with God" (John 5:18 NASB).
- "Looking for the blessed hope and the appearing of the glory of our Great God and Saviour, Christ Jesus" (Titus 2:13 NASB).
- "From now on I am telling you before it comes to pass so that when it does occur, you may believe that I am He" (John 13:19 NASB).

Jesus Exercised Divine Works

Jesus' friends and enemies were constantly amazed at the works He performed. In John 10, Jesus claims, "I and the Father are one." Then when the Jews again attempted to stone Him, "Jesus answered them, 'I showed you many good works from the Father; for which of them are you stoning Me?' The Jews answered Him, 'For a good work we do not stone You, but for blasphemy; and because You, being a man, make Yourself out to be God'" (John 10:30-33 NASB).

Some of the works attributed to Christ as well as to God are:

1. Christ created all things (John 1:3, Colossians 1:6, Hebrews 1:10).
2. Christ upholds all things (Colossians 1:17, Hebrews 1:3).

3. Christ directs and guides the course of history (1 Corinthians 10:1-11).
4. Christ forgives sin (Mark 2:5-12, Colossians 3:13).
5. Christ bestows eternal life (John 10:28, 1 John 5:10).
6. Christ will raise the dead at the resurrection (John 11:25, John 5:21, 28, 29).
7. Christ will be the judge of all men in final judgment (John 5:22, 27, Matthew 25:31-46, 2 Corinthians 5:10).

One of these works drew an especially strong reaction from Jesus' critics, the religious leaders. This is number four: Christ forgives sin. Mark 2:5-12 reads:

"And Jesus seeing their faith said to the paralytic, 'My son, your sins are forgiven.'
But there were some of the scribes sitting there and reasoning in their hearts, 'Why does this man speak that way? He is blaspheming; who can forgive sins but God alone?'
And immediately Jesus, perceiving in His spirit that they were reasoning that way within themselves, said to them, 'Why are you reasoning about these things in your hearts? Which is easier, to say to the paralytic, "Your sins are forgiven;" or to say, "Arise, and take up your pallet and walk"? But in order that you may know that the Son of Man has authority on earth to forgive sins'—He said to the paralytic, 'I say to you, rise, take up your pallet and go home.'
And he rose and immediately took up the pallet and went out in the sight of all; so that they were all amazed and were glorifying God, saying, 'We have never seen anything like this.' "

Now, it's true that I can forgive the sins you commit against me, but that doesn't prove I'm God. So why does the fact that Christ forgives sin help prove He's God? Only God can forgive sins committed against Himself. Yet Christ claimed to forgive sins committed against God. Thus, by forgiving the paralytic his sins, Jesus makes one of His boldest claims to deity.

There are many other references to Jesus making divine claims which establish without a doubt that He believed Himself to be God.

Jesus Possessed Divine Attributes

By Demonstration

Jesus not only claimed to be God; He also demonstrated that He had the ability to do things that only God could do.

- Jesus exercised authority over nature.

    "And on that day, when evening had come, He said to them, 'Let us go over to the other side.'

    And leaving the multitude, they took Him along with them, just as He was, in the boat; and other boats were with Him.

    And there arose a fierce gale of wind, and the waves were breaking over the boat so much that the boat was already filling up.

    And He Himself was in the stern, asleep on the cushion; and they awoke Him and said to Him, 'Teacher, do You not care that we are perishing?'

    And being aroused, He rebuked the wind and said to the sea, 'Hush, be still.' And the wind died down and it became perfectly calm. And He said to them, 'Why are you so timid? How is it that you have no faith?'

    And they became very much afraid and said to one another, 'Who then is this, that even the wind and the sea obey Him?' " (Mark 4:35-41 NASB).

- Jesus reported events which occurred when He was far away from the scene.

    "Jesus saw Nathanael coming to Him, and said of him, 'Behold an Israelite indeed, in whom is no guile!'

    Nathanael said to Him, 'How do You know me?' Jesus answered and said to him, 'Before Philip called you, when you were under the fig tree, I saw you.'

    Nathanael answered Him, 'Rabbi, You are the Son of God; You are the King of Israel.'

    Jesus answered and said to him, 'Because I said to you that I saw you under the fig tree, do you believe? You shall see greater things than these'" (John 1: 47-50).

- Jesus knew the very thoughts of people.

"But He knew what they were thinking..." (Luke 6:8 NASB).

- Jesus had authority over life and death.

"And it came about soon afterwards, that He went to a city called Nain; and His disciples were going along with Him, accompanied by a large multitude.

Now as He approached the gate of the city, behold a dead man was being carried out, the only son of his mother, and she was a widow; and a sizable crowd from the city was with her.

And when the Lord saw her, He felt compassion for her, and said to her, 'Do not weep.'

And He came up and touched the coffin; and the bearers came to a halt. And He said, 'Young man, I say to you, arise!'

And the dead man sat up, and began to speak. And Jesus gave him back to his mother.

And fear gripped them all, and they began glorifying God, saying, 'A great prophet has arisen among us!' and, 'God has visited His people!'

And this report concerning Him went out all over Judea, and in all the surrounding district" (Luke 7: 11-17 NASB).

By Association

Not only did Christ demonstrate the ability to do the things only God could do, but the attributes which were attributed to God were also attributed to Jesus Christ. These attributes are found both in the Old Testament prophecies attributed to the Messiah, the Christ, and in the New Testament as direct references to Jesus. Old Testament prophecies which refer to Jesus Christ and His attributes can be examined in Chapter 9, in *Evidence That Demands a Verdict*. Here the direct New Testament references will be considered.

The customary division of the attributes of God into metaphysical and moral is assumed here.

As regards metaphysical attributes we may affirm firstly that God is self-existent; secondly that He is immense (or infinite). In regard to immensity or infinity He is eternal, unchangeable, omnipresent, omnipotent, perfect, incomprehensible, omniscient.

As regards moral attributes God is holy, true, loving, righteous, faithful and merciful. In these respects man differs from the ideal of manhood in the sense that He is the Author of these qualities. They are un-derived in Him. It will not be deemed necessary here to go beyond mere proof that all these attributes of God existed in Him. If the metaphysical attributes of God exist in Christ, then the moral attributes are un-derived and infinite in degree. Emphasis therefore will be laid on the metaphysical attributes.

Jesus' several statements of His oneness with the Father bear upon this subject, especially John 16:15, "All things whatsoever the Father hath are mine." This is a marvelous claim. This explains why in the previous verse (John 16:14) He could say that the work of the Holy Spirit is to glorify Christ: "He shall glorify me for he shall take of mine and shall declare it unto you." Beyond Christ there is nothing to know about the character of God (John 14:9).

- Christ possesses the metaphysical attributes of God. These attributes involve what might be called the essence of God. (The following is not an exhaustive list.)

  1. *Self-existence.*

     Christ has the quality that He is not dependent on anyone or anything for His existence, and all other life is dependent on Him. John 1:4 reads, "In Him was life." Jesus states in John 14:6, "I am the life." He does not say "I have" but "I am." There is no life from amoeba to archangel apart from Christ. These verses must be explained against the background of the name Jehovah (Yahweh) as explained in Exodus 3:13-15 and 6:2-9 (also see Colossians 1:15-23).

  2. *Eternal*

     When used of created things this adjective means without end. As used of God, of course, it means without beginning or end. Some clear evidence is found in 1 John 5:11, 20 – "And the witness is this, that God has given us eternal life, and this life is in His Son."

     "And we know that the Son of God has come, and has given us understanding, in order that we might know Him who is true, and we are in Him who is true, in His Son Jesus Christ. This is the true God and eternal life."

Also see John 8:35, 1 John 1:2, Micah 5:2 and Isaiah 8:6.

3. *All-knowing.*

This attribute, also known as omniscience, is the quality of having all knowledge. Biblical evidence for omniscience attributed to Christ is found in three areas.

First is the opinion of the disciples. "Now we know that You know all things, and have no need for anyone to question You; by this we believe that You came from God" (John 16:30 NASB). Also compare John 21:17.

Second, the testimony of Scripture. "But there are some of you who do not believe. For Jesus knew from the beginning who they were who did not believe, and who it was that would betray Him" (John 6:64 NASB). Also see John 2:23-25.

Third, from examples in Scripture. "But Jesus, aware of their reasonings, answered and said to them, "Why are you reasoning in your hearts?" (Luke 5:22 NASB) Also see John 4:16-19, John 21:6 and Matthew 17:24-27.

Often people refer to Matthew 24:36 as an exception, to illustrate that Christ was not all-knowing. However, many scholars, including Augustine, understand the word "know" here to mean "to make known or declare." This is a proper meaning of the text. Thus Jesus is stating that it is not among his instructions from the Father to make this known at this time (Shedd, *Dogmatic Theology II*, 276).

4. *All-powerful.*

This means God can do anything not forbidden by His divine nature. For example, God cannot sin, for He is holy and righteous. Allowing for this exception, God can do anything (Mark 10:27). Another name for this attribute is omnipotence.

Christ claimed equality with God in this area. "Jesus therefore answered and was saying to them, 'Truly, truly, I say to you, the Son can do nothing of Himself, unless it is something He sees the Father doing; for whatever the Father does, these things the Son also does in like manner'" (John 5:19 NASB).

Jesus is called the Almighty. "I am the Alpha and the Omega," says the Lord God, "who is and who was and who is to come, the Almighty" (Revelation 1:8 NASB). Compare this with Revelation 1:17, 18; 22:12, 13 and Isaiah 41:4.

5. *Present everywhere.*

This is commonly called omnipresence. This means God is everywhere, there is no place where He is not present. What is important here is to note this does not mean God is everything. Rather, He is everywhere. God is separate from His creation. "...teaching them to observe all that I commanded you; and lo, I am with you always, even to the end of the age" (Matthew 28:20 NASV).

- Christ possesses the moral attributes of God. These are attributes which deal with the character of God. Again, this list is not complete.

1. *Holy.*

This means that God is pure, He cannot sin, and is unspoiled by evil or sin either by act or nature. Christ also possesses this attribute. "And the angel answered and said to her, 'The Holy Spirit will come upon you, and the power of the Most High will overshadow you; and for that reason the holy offspring shall be called the Son of God'" (Luke 1:35 NASV).

2. *Truth.*

Truth is the quality of being consistent with your words and actions and having those words and actions correspond to the real world. Thus it means you never lie. Christ's claims were strong here. He not only claimed to know the truth, He claimed He was the truth. The truth can never lie.

"Jesus said to him, 'I am the way, and the truth, and the life; no one comes to the Father, but through Me'" (John 14:6 NASV). "And to the angel of the church in Philadelphia write: 'He who is holy, who is true, who has the key of David, who opens and no one will shut, and who shuts and no one opens, says this..." (Revelation 3:7 NASV).

3. *Love.*
This means that love, unconditional in its nature, is an attribute of God. Here again bold statements are made with regard to Christ's love. "For God so loved the world, that He gave His only begotten Son, that whoever believes in Him should not perish, but have eternal life" (John 3:16 NASV).

"A new commandment I give to you, that you love one another, even as I have loved you, that you also love one another. By this all men will know that you are My disciples, if you have love for one another" (John 13:34,35 NASV).

4. Righteous.
God is a righteous or just God. Righteousness means a standard. God's standard of love, justice, holiness is what He expects of us. Only God's righteous standard is acceptable to Him. If God is righteous and God can only accept righteous people before Him, yet He alone can be perfectly righteous, but Christ was accepted as our righteousness, as a perfect substitute...

"Much more then, having now been justified by His blood, we shall be saved from the wrath of God through Him" (Romans 5:9 NASV).

"For if by the transgression of the one, death reigned through the one, much more those who receive the abundance of grace and of the gift of righteousness will reign in life through the One, Jesus Christ.

"So then as through one transgression there resulted condemnation to all men; even so through one act of righteousness there resulted justification of life to all men.

"For as through the one man's disobedience the many were made sinners, even so through the obedience of the One the many will be made righteous.

"And the Law came in that the transgression might increase; but where sin increased, grace abounded all the more, that, as sin reigned in death, even so grace might reign through righteousness to eternal life through Jesus Christ our Lord" (Romans 5:1 7-21 NASV).

"My little children, I am writing these things to you that you may not sin. And if anyone sins, we have an Advocate with the Father, Jesus Christ the righteous" (1 John 2:1 NASV).

"...in the future there is laid up for me the crown of righteousness, which the Lord, the righteous Judge, will award to me on that day; and not only to me, but also to all who have loved his appearing" (2 Timothy 4:8 NASV).—Then Christ's righteous sacrifice demonstrates His deity by His acceptance by God.

Now, concerning the moral attributes, some say, "I love unconditionally" or "I tell the truth, but that doesn't make me God." So why does it make Christ God? This question is answered by understanding two concepts, one having to do with God's nature, the other with our nature.

God's attributes are qualities that are all true of God and do not exist in isolation. In other words God's justice exists with God's love. One does not exclude the other. Thus, the attributes which represent the character of God are affected by those qualities which are true of His essence.

So if God is love and God is infinite (another attribute not touched on here) then God's love is infinite. This is in contrast to man. Man may love, but his love is not infinite.

Second, man's basic nature is sinful and has the tendency to continue to sin. Thus although man may act righteously at times, on his own, or may love unconditionally, ultimately he is bounded by and infected with his sin nature which results in disobedience to God's standard.

Jesus Received Worship as God

Jesus allowed Himself to be worshipped, something that is reserved for God alone.

- "You shall fear only the Lord your God; and you shall worship Him, and swear by His name" (Deuteronomy 6:13 NASB).

- "Then Jesus said to Him, 'Begone, Satan! For it is written, you shall worship the Lord your God, and serve Him only'" (Matthew 4:10 NASB).

- "Where is He who has been born King of the Jews? For we saw His star in the East, and have come to worship Him...And they came into the house and saw the child with Mary His mother; and they fell down and worshipped Him" (Matthew 2:2,11 NASB).

- "And behold, Jesus met them and greeted them. And they came up and took hold of His feet and worshipped Him" (Matthew 28:9)

- "And when they saw Him, they worshipped Him" (Matthew 28:17)

- "And he said, 'Lord, I believe.' And he worshipped Him" (John 9:38).

James Bjornstad, director of the Institute for Contemporary Christianity, makes an important observation:

To worship any other God, whether angel, man or manmade image is idolatry. In Colossians 2 we are warned, "Let no one keep defrauding you of your prize by delighting in...the worship of the angels" (Colossians 2:18).

We are not to worship angels and this is consistently demonstrated throughout the Bible. In Revelation 19:10 an angel (see 18:1) refuses worship from John. In Revelation 22:8,9, an angel refuses John's worship a second time, saying, "Do not do that...worship God."

Furthermore, Romans 1 explains that fools "exchanged the glory of the incorruptible God for an image in the form of corruptible man" (Romans 1:23). Obviously, we are not to worship man either. This, too, is consistently demonstrated throughout the Bible. In Acts 10:25,26, Peter refuses worship from Cornelius. In Acts 14:11-15, Paul and Barnabas refuse worship at Lystra.

From this evidence we can conclude that neither angels nor men are to be worshiped. Yet Jesus is worshiped, as we shall see, because He is God. He is not an angel or mere man. He is

God, and God alone is to be worshiped. (James Bjornstad, *Counterfeits At Your Door*, G/L Publications, 1979, pp. 21, 22.)

Jesus Is God Yahweh
Attributes ascribed to Yahweh in the Old Testament are also used in reference to Jesus in the New Testament, demonstrating that Jesus is Yahweh.

"THERE IS ONE GOD" 1 Corinthians 8:6

GOD IS...	YAHWEH IS JESUS	....JESUS IS
Genesis 1:1 Job 33:4 Isaiah 40:28	CREATOR	John 1:1-3 Colossians 1:12-17 Hebrews 1:8-12
Isaiah 41:4 Isaiah 44:6 Isaiah 48:12	FIRST & LAST	Revelation 1:17 Revelation 2:8 Revelation 22:13
Exodus 3:13,14 Deuteronomy 32:39 Isaiah 43:10	I AM (EGO EIMI)	John 8:24,58 John 13:19 John 18:5
Genesis 18:25 Psalm 96:13 Joel 3:12	JUDGE	2 Timothy 4:1 2 Corinthians 5:10 Romans 14:10-12
Psalm 47 Isaiah 44:6-8 Jeremiah 10:10	KING	Matthew 2:1-6 John 19:21 1 Timothy 6:13-16
Psalm 27:1 Isaiah 60:20	LIGHT	John 1:9 John 8:12
Psalm 106:21 Isaiah 43:3,11 Isaiah 45:21-23	SAVIOUR	John 4:42 Acts 4:10-12 1 John 4:14
Psalm 23 Psalm 100:3 Isaiah 40:11	SHEPHERD	John 10:11 Hebrews 13:20 1 Peter 5:4

(Ibid. p.89)

The teaching on the person of Jesus Christ from the Scripture is very clear. He was fully God and at the same time fully man. Any deviation from this position is not only unscriptural, it is also heretical. Those who attempt to make Jesus something less than God cannot go to the Bible for their justification. Therefore, if one takes the Bible seriously, one must conclude that Jesus of Nazareth was God in human flesh.

For further material and sources see *More Than a Carpenter*, chapter 1 and *Evidence That Demands a Verdict*, chapter 6.

The Doctrine of the Church

The Westminster Confession of Faith contains a statement about the church that is accepted by all branches of Christendom.

> The catholic or universal Church, which is invisible, consists of the whole number of the elect, that have been, are, or shall be gathered into one, under Christ the head thereof, and is the spouse, the body, the fullness of Him that filleth all in all. The visible Church, which is also catholic or universal under the gospel (not confined to one nation, as before under the law), consists of all those, throughout the world, that profess the true religion, and of their children, and is the kingdom of the Lord Jesus Christ, the house and family of God, out of which there is no ordinary possibility of salvation.

The true church is made up of all those individuals who have put their trust in Christ as their Savior. It is not merely the attending of church or having a name on the membership list that makes on a member of Christ's true church. Only the transforming work of the Holy Spirit in the heart of the repentant sinner qualifies one for membership in the true body of Christ.

The Atonement

Within all branches of Christianity there is agreement that the deity of Christ was a perfect satisfaction to God as just and substitutionary punishment for the sins of the world:

> Therefore as in Adam we had fallen under sin, the curse, and death, so we are delivered from sin, the curse, and death in Jesus Christ. His voluntary suffering and death on the cross for us, being of infinite value and merit, as the death of one sinless, God and man in one person, is both a perfect

satisfaction to the justice of God, which had condemned us for sin to death, and a fund of infinite merit, which has obtained him the right, without prejudice to justice, to give us sinners pardon of our sins, and grace to have victory over sin and death (The longer catechism of the Eastern Orthodox Church, answer to question 208).

Doctrine of Salvation

The doctrine of salvation is linked with the atoning death of Christ on the cross. While all major branches of Christianity agree that Christ's death was satisfactory to God as a sacrifice for the world's sins, there is a disagreement on how that sacrifice is appropriated. We believe the Bible teaches that salvation is by grace, a free gift of God to all those who believe in Christ. Those who receive Christ by faith have their sins forgiven and become children of God, a new creation in Christ Jesus:

> "For by grace you have been saved through faith; and that not of yourselves, it is the gift of God; not as a result of works, that no one should boast" (Ephesians 2:8, 9 NASB).

> "He saved us, not on the basis of deeds which we have done in righteousness but according to His mercy, by the washing of regeneration and renewing by the Holy Spirit" (Titus 3:5 NASB).

> "But as many as received Him, to them He gave the right to become children of God, even to those who believe in His name" (John 1:12 NASB).

> "In Him we have redemption through His blood, the forgiveness of our trespasses, according to the riches of His grace" (Ephesians 1:7 NASB).

> "Therefore if any man is in Christ, he is a new creature; the old things are passed away; behold, new things have come" (2 Corinthians 5:17 NASB).

Since salvation is a free gift from God, no one can add anything to the completed work of Christ to receive it. It is received by faith and faith alone.

The Doctrine of Man

The Doctrine of Man is succinctly expressed in the Westminster Shorter Catechism, that "God created man, male and female, after his own image, in knowledge, righteousness, and holiness, with dominion over the creatures."

Francis Schaeffer, contemporary Christian philosopher, elaborates on what it means for modern man to be created in the image of God:

> What is it that differentiates Adam and Eve from the rest of creation? We find the answer in Genesis 1:26: "And God said, Let us make man in our image..." What differentiates Adam and Eve from the rest of creation is that they were created in the *image of God*. For twentieth-century man this phrase, *the image of God*, is as important as anything in Scripture, because men today can no longer answer this crucial question, "Who am I?" In his own naturalistic theories, with the uniformity of cause and effect in a closed system, with an evolutionary concept of a mechanical, chance parade from the atom to man, man has lost his unique identity. As he looks out upon the world, as he faces the machine, he cannot tell himself from what he faces. He cannot distinguish himself from other things.
>
> Quite in contrast, a Christian does not have this problem. He knows who he is. If anything is a gift of God, this is it — knowing who you are. As a Christian, I know my differentiation. I can look at the most complicated machine that men have made so far or ever will make and realize that, though the machine may do some things that I cannot do, I am different from it. If I see a machine that is stronger than I am, it doesn't matter. If it can lift a house, I am not disturbed. If it can run faster than I can, its speed doesn't threaten me. If I am faced with a giant computer which can never be beaten when it plays checkers — even when I realize that never in history will I or any man be able to beat it — I am not crushed. Others may be overwhelmed intellectually and psychologically by the fact that a man can make a machine that can beat him at his own games, but not the Christian" (Francis Schaeffer, *Genesis in Space and Time*, InterVarsity Press, 1972, pp. 46-47).

The Deity of the Holy Spirit

Central to the Christian faith is the teaching that the Holy Spirit is personal and is God, the third person of the Holy Trinity. The doctrine that the Holy Spirit is a person is clearly taught in Scripture. Notice the following examples of personal attributes displayed by the Holy Spirit. He can be grieved (Ephesians 4:30), resisted (Acts 7:51) and lied to (Acts 5:3). Moreover, the Holy Spirit can speak (Acts 21:11), think (Acts 15:28) and teach (Luke 12:12). Thus, the Holy Spirit is personal.

Furthermore, the Holy Spirit is spoken of in the Bible as a divine person. The Holy Spirit has the attributes of God, for He is all-powerful (Luke 1:35-37), eternal (Hebrews 9:14), and all-knowing (1 Corinthians 2:10,11). The Scriptures teach that lying to the Holy Spirit is lying to God (Acts 5:3,4).

The Holy Spirit also was involved in divine works, including creation (Genesis 1:2, Job 33:4), the new birth (John 3:5), the resurrection of Christ (Romans 8:11) and the inspiration of the Bible (2 Peter 1:20,21). Finally, to blaspheme against the Holy Spirit is an unforgivable sin (Matthew 12:31,32). The conclusion is that the Holy Spirit is God, the third person of the Holy Trinity.

Conclusion

As Bible-believing Christians, we know that God is personal, eternal and triune. However, the cults each deny one or more of the essential Bible doctrines we have discussed. Beware of any group or individual that changes essential doctrines. The Bible's teachings cannot be exploited at the whim of any group or individual. It contains "the faith once for all delivered to the saints" (Jude 3) and one who changes its divine pronouncements acts like those condemned in 2 Peter 3:16: "The untaught and unstable distort, as they do also the rest of the Scriptures, to their own destruction."

CHAPTER FOUR

Hare Krishna

History

The origin of the Hare Krishnas (International Society for Krishna Consciousness or ISKCON) dates back to the fifteenth century A.D., when Chaitanya Mahaprabhu developed The Doctrines of Krishnaism from the Hindu sect of Vishnuism.

Simply stated, Vishnuism believed Vishnu, the Supreme God, manifested himself at one time as Krishna. Chaitanya Mahaprabhu taught the reverse: Krishna was the chief God who had revealed himself at one time as Vishnu. The doctrinal system of Krishnaism is Hinduistic and denies personality in God's ultimate state while believing every individual must go through a series of successive lives (reincarnation) to rid himself of the debt of his actions (karma).

Krishnaism was one of the early attempts to make philosophical Hinduism appealing to the masses. While pure Hinduism's god is impersonal and unknowable, Krishnaism (and other sects) personalize god and promote worship of and interaction with the personalized aspects of god, such as Krishna.

In 1965 Krishnaism came to America by means of Abhay Charan De Bhaktivedanta Swami Prabhupada, an aged Indian exponent of the worship of Krishna. He founded ISKCON and remained its leader until his death in 1978. Presently, ISKCON is ruled by two different groups, one group of eleven men rule over spiritual matters, while a board of directors heads the administrative matters. This wealthy organization presently has about 10,000 members in America. Part of ISKCON's wealth comes from soliciting funds and distributing its lavishly illustrated literature including the *Bhagavad-Gita: As It Is* and its periodical *Back to Godhead*.

ISKCON's beliefs are those of Hinduism and are wholly incompatible with Christianity. This can be observed by a comparison between the statements of ISKCON on matters of belief with those of the Bible.

God

The Bible speaks of God as the infinite-personal creator of the universe. He is eternally a separate entity from His creation. He existed before His creation came into being. The Scripture says, "In the beginning God created the heavens and the earth" (Genesis 1:1), showing God was there before His creation existed.

In contrast to this, ISKCON, along with other Hindu sects, makes no ultimate and real distinction between God the creator and His creation. To them they are all one. "In the beginning of the creation, there was only the Supreme Personality Narayana. There was no Brahma, no Siva, no fire, no moon, no stars in the sky, no sun. There was only Krishna, who creates all and enjoys all.

"All the lists of the incarnations of Godhead are either plenary expansions or parts of the plenary expansions of the Lord, but Lord Sri Krsna (alternate spelling of Krishna) is the original Personality of Godhead Himself," Srimad Bhagauatam 1:3:28 (Bhaktivenda Book Trust, n.d.).

Jesus Christ

According to Scripture, Jesus Christ is God Almighty who became a man in order to die for the sins of the world. He has been God from all eternity. "In the beginning was the Word and the Word was with God and the Word was God" (John 1:1).

ISKCON denies this by making Christ no more than Krishna's son. "Jesus is the son, and Krsna is the Father, and Jesus is Krsna's son" (*Jesus Loves Krsna*, Los Angeles Bhaktivenda Book Trust, n.d., p. 26).

Salvation

The Bible teaches that all of us have sinned against a holy God and are therefore in need of a Savior: "For all have sinned and come short of the glory of God" (Romans 3:23); "For the wages of sin is death but the gift of God is eternal life through Jesus Christ our Lord" (Romans 6:23).

This is not so in the teachings of ISKCON. According to ISKCON, salvation must be earned by performing a series of works.

To get rid of the ignorance, one must practice disciplinary devotion by chanting the name of God, hearing and singing his praises, meditating upon the divine play and deeds of KRSNA, and engaging in the rites and ceremonies of worship. One must also repeat the name of God to the count of beads (Abhay Charan de Bhaktivedanta Swami Prabhupada, *Bhagavad-Gita As It Is* p. 326).

Self-denial and sacrifice are crucial for salvation in ISKCON. Note the following quotation,

> All these performers who know the meaning of sacrifice become cleansed of sinful reactions, and, having tasted the nectar of the remnants of such sacrifices, they go to the supreme eternal atmosphere (ibid p. 81).

The Passantinos have done extensive research in the area of the cults, and they offer pertinent comments regarding salvation in ISKCON:

> Salvation in Hare Krishna is thoroughly entwined with the Hindu concept of karma, or retributive justice. This teaching, which requires belief in reincarnation and/or transmigration of the soul, says that one's deeds, good and bad, are measured and judged either for or against him. Only when his good deeds have "atoned" for his bad deeds (and he is thus cleansed of this evil world) can he realize his oneness with Krishna and cease his cycles of rebirth.
>
> The idea of karma and reincarnation is anti-biblical. Is it just or reasonable for a man to suffer in this life or be required to atone for sins in this life that he committed in a previous life that he doesn't even remember? How can suffering for an unknown sin reform the sinner and mature him to the point where he no longer performs that sin? Such so-called justice is cruel and absolutely opposed to the God of the Bible (Robert and Gretchen Passantino, op. cit., p. 150).

Conclusion

Since ISKCON has a different God, a different Jesus, and a different way of salvation from what the Bible reveals, it is impossible for there to be any compatibility between the two. They differ on all crucial issues. A person must choose between Krishna and Jesus Christ; no harmony can exist between the sect of Hare Krishna and Christianity.

Hare Krishna Terms

ISKCON—Acronym for the official name for the Hare Krishna movement: The International Society for Krishna Consciousness.

Prabhupada, A. C. Bhaktivedanta—Late founder and spiritual head of ISKCON, a religious philosophy of self-denial where the devotees stress asceticism to attain God-consciousness. Born in India in 1896, he came to America in 1965 with the message of Krishna. He was considered by his devotees as Krishna's representative on earth.

Back to Godhead—The best-known of the Hare Krishna (ISKCON) publications.

Bhakti Yoga—The type of yoga, or exercise to spirituality, practiced by Hare Krishnas.

Karma—The Hindu idea of one's accumulated debts (bad deeds). Karma must be paid for during an individual's succession of lives (reincarnation).

Karmis—The Hare Krishna term for non-members, who are said to be captives of their own bad karma.

Laksmi—The Hare Krishna term for money. Also the name of one of the Hindu god Krishna's consorts.

Mantra—The Hindu prayer chant, specialized for each Hindu sect, including the Hare Krishnas.

Nirvana—The Hindu concept of heaven or bliss.

Paramatma—The Hare Krishna term for the Holy Spirit.

Sankirtana—The mantra, or religious chant in the Hare Krishna movement. Chanting of the Sankirtana "brings one ever closer to God-consciousness."

CHAPTER FIVE

Jehovah's Witnesses

History

Officially known as the Watchtower Bible and Tract Society, the Jehovah's Witnesses are a product of the life work of Charles Taze Russell, born February 16, 1852, near Pittsburgh, Pennsylvania. In 1870, while still in his teens and without formal theological education, Russell organized a Bible class whose members eventually made him "pastor:"

In 1879 he founded the magazine *Zion's Watchtower* in which he published his own unique interpretation of the Bible, and in 1886, the first volume of seven books (six written by Russell) entitled *The Millennial Dawn* was published (later retitled *Studies in the Scriptures*). .

By the time of his death in 1916, "Pastor" Russell, according to the Watchtower, traveled more than a million miles, gave more than thirty thousand sermons, and wrote books totalling over fifty thousand pages (*Qualified to be Ministers*, Anon., 1955, p. 310).

Joseph F. Rutherford

A few months after the death of Charles Taze Russell, the society's legal counselor, Joseph Franklin Rutherford, became the second President of the Watchtower Society. It was under his leadership that the name "Jehovah's Witnesses" was adopted. Rutherford not only moved the Society's headquarters to Brooklyn, he also moved toward "theocratic" control with the power to make all policy decisions.

Nathan Knorr

Rutherford died in 1942 and was succeeded by Nathan H. Knorr. It was during Knorr's presidency that the society increased from 115,000 to over two million members. In 1961, under Knorr's leadership, the society produced its own English translation of the Bible entitled *The New World Translation of Holy Scriptures.*

When Knorr died in 1977, Frederick W. Franz became the new president of the Watchtower and is currently conducting business in Knorr's manner. Franz was the spokesman for the translation committee of the New World Translation, although he has no recognized qualifications as a translator of either Hebrew or Greek.

Claims of the Jehovah's Witnesses

Today, worldwide, the Jehovah's Witnesses number over two million. The members are zealous and sincere and claim to accept the Bible as their only authority. However, their theology denies every cardinal belief of historic Christianity including the Trinity, the divinity of Jesus Christ, His bodily resurrection, salvation by grace through faith, and eternal punishment of the wicked.

"Pastor" Russell, not known for his humility, made the following statement, "Be it known that no other system of theology even claims, or has ever attempted to harmonize in itself every statement of the Bible, yet nothing short of this can we claim" (Charles Taze Russell *Studies in the Scriptures,* 1:348). The Watchtower has this to say about itself:

> It is God's sole collective channel for the flow of Biblical truth to men on earth (*The Watchtower,* July 15, 1960, p. 439).
>
> The Watchtower Bible and Tract Society is the greatest corporation in the world, because from the time of its organization until now the Lord has used it as His channel through which to make known the glad tidings (*The Watchtower,* 1917, p. 22, quoted in *Studies in the Scriptures,* p. 144).
>
> F.W. Franz, president of the Watchtower, relaying how

their interpretations come from God, stated, "They are passed to the Holy Spirit who invisibly communicates with Jehovah's Witnesses — and the Publicity Department" (*Scottish Daily Express*, November 24, 1954).

We conclude from these statements that the Watchtower believes itself to be *the* organization that speaks for God in today's world. Note the following statement by "Pastor" Russell:

> If the six volumes of "Scripture Studies" are practically the Bible, topically arranged with Bible proof texts given, we might not improperly name the volumes "the Bible in an arranged form," that is to say, they are not mere comments on the Bible, but they are practically the Bible itself. Furthermore, not only do we find that people cannot see the divine plan in studying the Bible by itself, but we see, also, that if anyone lays the *Scripture Studies* aside, even after he has used them, after he has become familiar with them, after he has read them for ten years—if he then lays them aside and ignores them and goes to the Bible alone, though he has understood his Bible for ten years, our experience shows that within two years he goes into darkness. On the other hand, if he had merely read the *Scripture Studies* with their references and had not read a page of the Bible as such, he would be in the light at the end of two years, because he would have the light of the Scriptures (Charles Taze Russell, *The Watchtower*, September 15, 1910, p. 298).

Source of Authority

There are no "articles of faith" or authoritative doctrinal statements issued by the Watchtower. Their theological views are found in their various publications, including *The Watchtower* and *Awake*. The doctrine that proceeds from these works is considered authoritative.

They contend their ultimate source of authority is the Bible:

> To let God be found true means to let God have the say as to what is the truth that sets men free. It means to accept His Word, the Bible, as the truth. Hence, in this book, our appeal is to the Bible for the truth. Our obligation is to back up what is said herein by quotations from the Bible for proof of truthfulness and reliability (*Let God Be True*, 1946, p. 9).

Although the Watchtower contends that the Scriptures are their final authority, we find they constantly misuse the Scriptures to establish their own peculiar beliefs. This is accomplished chiefly by quoting texts out of context while omitting other passages relevant to the subject. For all practical purposes their publications take precedence over the Scriptures.

Trinity

The Watchtower makes it clear they do not believe in the doctrine of the Trinity. "The trinity doctrine was not conceived by Jesus or the early Christians" (*Let God Be True*, 1952, p. 92). "The plain truth is that this is another of Satan's attempts to keep the God-fearing person from learning the truth of Jehovah and His Son Christ Jesus" (*Let God Be True*, p. 93).

In Watchtower theology neither Jesus Christ nor the Holy Spirit is God.

Jesus Christ

In the theological system of the Jehovah's Witnesses, Jesus Christ is not God in human flesh, but rather a created being.

"Jesus, the Christ, a created individual, is the second greatest personage of the Universe. Jehovah God and Jesus together constitute the superior authorities" (*Make Sure of All Things*, p. 207).

...."He was a god, but not the Almighty God, who is Jehovah" (*Let God Be True*, p. 33).

"If Jesus were God, then during Jesus' death God was dead in the grave" (*Let God Be True*, 1946, p. 91).

"The truth of the matter is that the word is Christ Jesus, who did have a beginning" (*Let God Be True*, p. 88).

The denial of the deity of Christ is nothing new in the history of the Church. It is a revival of the ancient heresy known as Arianism (named after the fourth century A.D. heretic Arius.) Arianism teaches that the Son was of a substance different than the Father and was, in fact, created).

To the Jehovah's Witnesses, Jesus is not equal to Jehovah God. He was rather, Michael the Archangel in his preexistent state, having a brother named Lucifer who rebelled against God while he (known then as Michael) remained obedient (see J. Rutherford, *The Kingdom Is At Hand*, p. 49).

During his earthly existence Michael was transformed into a man:

> "The life of the Son of God was transferred from his glorious position with God his Father in Heaven to the embryo of a human" (*Let God Be True*, p. 36).

Upon His resurrection He went back to His former state as an invisible spirit, no longer having a body, according to Jehovah's Witnesses' theology.

The Jehovah's Witnesses, in an attempt to demonstrate that Jesus Christ is not Jehovah God, appeal to the Bible to substantiate their beliefs. However, it is the Bible that contradicts their theology, revealing it to be both unbiblical and non-Christian.

John 14:28

One favorite passage used by Jehovah's Witnesses to prove Christ is less than God is John 14:28: "My Father is greater than I." This verse refers to the voluntary subordination of Jesus during His earthly life when He willingly placed Himself in submission to the Father. It says nothing about His nature, only His temporary rank on earth. Thus, the "greater than" refers to His position rather than His person.

Revelation 3:14

One of the crucial phrases the Watchtower Society uses to support its doctrine of the creation of Christ is the latter part of Revelation 3:14, "...the beginning (αϱχη) of the creation of God." It is used in their extended work on *"The Word" Who is He? According to John* to set forth that the Lord was a product of the creative activity of God. "Plainly it means the first one or original one of God's ways to be created." (*"The Word" Who is He? According to John* [Brooklyn: Watchtower Bible and Tract Society, 1962], p. 47.)

The Watchtower, which proclaims the authentic doctrinal views of the Watchtower Bible and Tract Society, states with reference to Revelation 3:14:

This is true because his firstborn Son was the first of God's creations. Then with him as His active agent God went on to create everything else that has been brought into existence. He was the "beginning of the creation of God," not that he was the author of creation, but that he was the first one whom God made and whom God made without the co-operation of anyone else. ("Resurrection to a New World," *The Watchtower*, 68:99, April 1, 1947.)

Grammatically, there are two ways in which to understand this phrase: "...the beginning of the creation of God." It might be interpreted passively of Christ as the "beginning of the creation of God," as the first and most excellent creature of God's hands, or, it might declare of Christ, "that He was the active source, author, and in this sense, *'beginning'* and beginner of all creation; as in the words of the Creed, 'by whom all things were made.'" (Trench, *Seven Churches*, pp. 256-57.)

Although both meanings are possible if merely considered as entities, but with reference to the many statements of Scripture concerning Christ's deity, the latter is imperatively demanded. The Catholic Church rejected the former interpretation because it would "place this passage in contradiction with every passage in Scripture which claims divine attributes..." (*Ibid.*, p. 257.)

The *New World Translation of the Christian Greek Scriptures* is in error at this point by rendering this portion of the verse, "...the beginning of the creation by God." The genitive case means, "of God" and not, "by God."

Bruce Metzger points out if the passage were to teach that Christ was created "by God" it would have required the preposition "hupo" rather than "tou theou" which means "of God" (*Theology Today*, Bruce Metzger, 1953, pp. 79-80).

One need go no farther than these seven church letters referred to above by Trench. All the titles given to Christ by Himself are either divine or consistent with His divinity.

Several expressions of Paul to the Colossians are prototypes of certain phrases of John in Revelation. Paul wrote an epistle to the Laodiceans (Colossians 4:16) and gave directions for the Colossian epistle to be read in the church of Laodicea. The message inscribed by St. John to the Laodicean Church continues the theme commenced by St. Paul to the Colossians. It is highly probable that John was acquainted with Paul's epistle and was aware of the Laodicean problem. Lightfoot's remarks here are pertinent to this discussion:

> Thus, while St. Paul finds it necessary to enforce the truth that Christ is the image of the invisible God, that in Him all the divine fullness dwells, that He existed before all things, that through Him all things were created and in Him all thinbgs are sustained, that He is the primary source (αϱχη) and has the pre-eminence in all things; so in almost identical language St. John, speaking in the person of our Lord, declares that He is the Amen, the faithful and true witness, the primary source (αϱχη) of the creation of God.
>
> Some lingering shreds of the old heresy, we may suppose, still hung about these Churches, and instead of "holding fast the Head" they were even yet prone to substitute intermediate agencies, angelic mediators, as links in the chain which should bind man to God. They still failed to realize the majesty and significance, the completeness, of the Person of Christ. (Lightfoot, *Colossians*, pp. 41-42.)

Wordsworth corroborates the above statement of Lightfoot's that "...there may be some reference to the false teaching of those at Laodicea who substituted *Angels* as *Creators* and *Mediators* in the place of Christ." (Chr. Wordsworth, *The New Testament of our Lord and Saviour Jesus Christ, in the Original Greek*, p. 180.)

A few years before John's letter, Laodicea had been laid waste by an earthquake. After this catastrophe she was rebuilt better than her former splendor. She boasted that she did it herself, without the assistance of the Roman emperor (Lightfoot, *Colossians*, p. 43.). In Revelation 3:17, 18, John condemned this pride of wealth. Christ gave Himself this name in the Epistle, so that they would rely on Him for their salvation and not look for any good thing except from Him (Revelation 3:18).

The Laodiceans were probably familiar with this term, "beginning of the creation of God," as meaning the originating source through whom God works. Revelation 1:18; 2:8; 3:21; and 5:15 are passages that make it clear this concept in Colossians 1:15-18; John 1:3; and Hebrews 1:2

was well known to the Laodiceans. Christ is presented as the unqualified medium of the whole creation.

The Lord, in the other passages of Revelation, refers to Himself as not only the "Beginning," but the "End." (See also: Revelation 1:8; 21:6; 22:13; compare with 1:17; 2:8; Isaiah 41:4; 44:6; 48:12). Christ is the end to which all creation tends. Christ is also called the "Amen," and the "faithful and true Witness," in Revelation 3:14. The Amen seems to refer to Isaiah 65:16 where the "God of Amen," was translated in the LXX (The Septuagint) as, the God of truth..."

"The Amen" signifies the truth of His promises and "the true witness" points to the validity of His revelations of heaven, earthly things, and the purpose and nature of God (See also: John 1:3; 3:11, 12; 8:28, 29; 10:28; 14:9). Revelation 3:14 introduces a strong antithesis as a condemnation for the unfaithful and immature condition of the Church of Laodicea.

John refers to Christ as the beginning in the active sense: "the living beginning," the "first cause of creation." (Arndt and Gingrich, *A Greek-English Lexicon of the New Testament*, pp. 456-457). It signifies the causal relation of Christ to the creation of God.

A. T. Robertson, the Greek grammarian had this to say: "Not the first of creatures as the Arians held and Unitarians do now, but the originating source of creation through whom God works" (*Word Pictures in the New Testament*, Vol. VI, p. 321).

ἀρχή, as the "source of creation," not only coincides with the historical and etymological use of the word, but also the context and scriptural teaching about Christ. The Watchtower Society, in its strict adherence to this verse in order to verify a created beginning for Christ, not only disregards a thorough exegesis of ἀρχή but also ignores the overall biblical teaching.

Proverbs 8:22

The interpretation of Proverbs 8:22 has raised a greater controversy than almost any other passage in the Old Testament (F. C. Burney, "Christ as the APXH of Creation," *Journal of Theological Studies*, 27:160, 1926). This is a verse the Jehovah's Witnesses (along with Arians of every age) appeal to most frequently to confirm their view that Jesus Christ was a created Being (Bruce M. Metzger, "The Jehovah's Witnesses and Jesus Christ," *Theology Today*, 15:80, April, 1953). Their own Bible, *The New World Translation of the Hebrew Scriptures* (*New World Translation of the Holy Scriptures* [Brooklyn: Watchtower Bible and Tract Society, 1963].) purportedly rendered from the original languages by the New World Bible translation committee, translates Proverbs 8:22 as follows:

> Jehovah himself produced me as the beginning of his way, the earliest of his achievements of long ago.

A footnote makes reference to the meaning "to create." (*Ibid.*, p. 1945.)

Their teaching on Christ being a created being with reference to Proverbs 8:22 permeates many of their publications. *The Watchtower*, the authoritative voice of the society (Also known as: *Millennial Dawn. Watchtower Bible and Tract Society. The People's Pulpit Association. The International Bible Student's Association*, etc.), states:

> What then was his first creation? a son—his first son... ("Wise Sayings for the Modern Day," *Watchtower*, 78:659, November 1, 1957.) This created son of God... (*Ibid.*, p. 660.) ...before he created his wise son... (*Ibid.*, p. 662.)

In their book, *What Has Religion Done for Mankind?*, it reads:

> In the proverbs of wisdom, he speaks of himself as wisdom and calls attention to his being a creation of the eternal heavenly Father. (*What Has Religion Done for Mankind?* [Brooklyn: Watchtower Bible and Tract Society, Inc., 1951], p. 37.)

"The Word": Who Is He? According to John mentions that Proverbs 8:22,

> does not mean Beginner, Origin, or Originator. Plainly, it means the first one or original one of God's ways to be created. (*"The Word": Who is He? According to John* [Brooklyn: Watchtower Bible and Tract Society, Inc., 1962], p. 47.)

There is no doubt that the Witnesses teach from this Old Testament verse the creation of Christ.

The pivotal point of the controversy centers on the Hebrew word *ganah*. The basic meaning of the word here should be understood as "beget," or "create," not to "produce" as translated by the Watchtower. The lexicons, the biblical usage, substantives derived from the root word, extra-biblical literature, the cognate languages, the early versions and the context of the Bible, all support the biblical usage and not the Watchtower.

The context is the critical stage in the exegesis of the passage. The decision whether הֶנָק means "to create," or "to beget," ultimately must be based upon the meanings of the verbs descriptive of the production of wisdom in the immediate context of Proverbs 8:22-25.

In Proverbs 8:23, "set up" means "I was woven" (prenatal growth of the embryo) and verses 24, 25 means "I was brought forth with travail" (birth). The conclusion is obvious that the verb "set up" in verse 22 is "beget me" (act of procreation). The above discussion of Proverbs 8:22-25 is summed up adequately by Kidner when he said that, "the passage as a whole may be meant to bring to mind a 'royal' birth." (Derek Kidner, *The Proverbs*, p. 8).

Colossians 1:15

Jesus is called the "firstborn" of all creation in Colossians 1:15. The Watchtower takes this to mean "first created." However, the passage itself states that Christ is the Creator of all things (vs. 16, 17), not a created being. The title firstborn refers to His preeminent position, not that he is Jehovah's "first creation."

The meaning of "firstborn" in Colossians 1:15 is perhaps impossible, or at least difficult, to understand without an accurate understanding of its Old Testament implications. The Hebrew term specifies the firstborn of human beings as well as animals (Exodus 11:5). A word from the same root denotes firstfruits (Exodus 23:16). This rendering "firstfruits," may mean the "first ripe" or "choicest" of the fruit.

Firstborn was a term applied in the Mosaic Law concerning the specific rights and obligations of the first male child of a family (Louis Hartman, *Encyclopedic Dic-*

tionary of The Bible [New York: McGraw-Hill Book Co., Inc., 1963], p. 777). The firstborn of the father had the right of primogeniture: he acquired a special blessing (Genesis 27); he became heir of a double share of the father's wealth (Deuteronomy 21:17); he replaced his father as head of the family and, therefore, possessed authority over the younger brothers and sisters (Genesis 27:29-40; 49:8; *Ibid.*, p. 778). Primogeniture involved representation of the father in the civil as well as religious capacity.

The firstborn was believed to possess a specific precedence in holiness since through him flowed the common blood of the tribe (Genesis 49:3; Deuteronomy 21:17). (I. Benzinger, "Family and Marriage Relations, Hebrew," *The New Schaff-Herzog Encyclopedia of Religious Knowledge* [New York: Funk and Wagnalls Company, 1908], IV, 277). This importance attached to the firstborn was believed to indicate a priesthood relating to the eldest sons of the families. (John McClintock and James Strong, "First-born," *Cyclopedia of Biblical, Theological and Ecclesiastical Literature* [New York: Harper and Brothers, 1873], III, 571.) This eminence was inferred from the particular claim of Yahweh to all the firstborn (Exodus 22:29). (Benzinger, *ibid.*).

Casanowicz, writing in *The Jewish Encyclopedia*, notes that the prerogatives of the firstborn consisted of: (1) a kind of *potestad* over the family; (2) a double share of inheritance; (3) the right of the priesthood; (4) God's promises to the patriarchs were considered as attached to the line of the firstborn (I. M. Casanowicz, "Primogeniture," *The Jewish Encyclopedia* [New York: Funk and Wagnalls Company, 1905], X, 198).

From the apparent regulations in the rabbinical law, Casanowicz concludes that "...the prerogative of primogeniture was not conceived as an inalienable right inherent in the firstborn, but rather as a gift by the law..." (*Ibid.*) Wine adds that the use of the term is not a reverence to birth but to position of favor. (W. B. Wine, *Epistles to the Philippians and Colossians* [London: Oliphant Limited, 1955], p. 135.)

After Reuben had forfeited his right of primogeniture, his priority in time was not passed on to Judah; but the dominion belonging to it was transferred to Judah and the double portion to Joseph (1 Chronicles 5:2).

This conclusion is also evident in the case of Esau and Jacob (Genesis 25:23-33). Jacob purchased the birthright from Esau, but he could not purchase Esau's priority in time. Another case in which the birthright was transferred is in the case of the Levites in Numbers 3:9:

> By destroying the firstborn of Egypt and sparing those of Israel, YHWH acquired an especial ownership over the latter. But as it was not feasible to select the firstborn of the entire nation and thus disturb the family organization, the Levites were substituted for them (Casanowicz, op. cit., p. 199).

It is apparent that to receive this supremacy one did not have to be born first. Rees concludes in *The International Standard Bible Encyclopedia* that

> the laws and customs of all nations show that to be "first-born" means, not only priority in time, but a certain superiority in privilege and authority (T. Rees, "First-Begotten," *The International Standard Bible Encyclopedia* [Grand Rapids: Wm. B. Eerdmans Publishing Company, 1960], II, 1113).

Firstborn is also rendered metaphorically in the Old Testament (Francis Brown, S. R. Driver, and Charles Briggs, *A Hebrew and English Lexicon of the Old Testament* [Oxford: Clarendon Press, 1955], p. 114). The term was used figuratively in Job 18:13, "the firstborn of death...". "The firstborn son," notes Fausset, "held the chief place (Genesis 49:3); so here *the chiefest (most deadly) disease* that death has ever engendered" (Robert Jamieson, A. Fausset, and David Brown, *A Commentary Critical, Experimental and Practical on the Old and New Testaments* [Grand Rapids: Wm. B. Eerdmans Publishing Co., 1961], III, 44). Another use parallel to the above is Isaiah 14:30, "and the firstborn of the poor shall feed..." This denotes the poorest of the poor, the "...most abject poor" (*Ibid.*, p. 612).

It is also applied in the Old Testament to Israel as the firstborn of God (Exodus 4:22; Jeremiah 31:9), implying Israel as "...the prerogative race" J. B. Lightfoot, *Saint Paul's Epistles to the Colossians and to Philemon* [Grand Rapids: Zondervan Publishing House, 1961], p. 146). This paved the way for the later Messianic reference to "first-born" as "the ideal representative of the race" (Thomas K. Abbott, *Epistles to the Ephesians and to the Colossians* [The International Critical Commentary. Grand Rapids: Wm. B. Eerdmans Publishing Company, 1957], p. 210).

Abbott indicates from the writings of Rabbi Nathan in *Shemoth Rabba*, on the interpretation of Psalms 89:27 (Psalms 89:28 in the LXX), that this term "seems to have been a recognized title of the Messiah (see Hebrews 1:6) (*Ibid*).

The title firstborn had been used so much as a title of sovereignty that God Himself is called "Firstborn of the world," by R. Bechai on the Pentateuch. (Lightfoot, *Colossians*, p. 47).

It may be ascertained from the above evidence that the use of "firstborn" in the Old Testament to mean "priority of birth" or "in time" has been overshadowed by and sometimes even lost in the idea of "supremacy" or "preeminence." This meaning may be distinctly seen in Genesis 49:3 where Jacob said of Reuben, "Thou art my firstborn, my might, and the beginning of my strength, the excellency of dignity, and the excellency of power." The dominating thought here is not primogeniture, but dignity, honor, strength and sovereignty.

It is used in Romans 8:29 to denote one who "... is chief, or who is highly distinguished and preeminent" (Albert Barnes, *Notes on the New Testament: Explanatory and Practical* [London: Blackie and Sons, 1851], VII, 246). Arndt and Gingrich use it figuratively "of Christ, as the firstborn of a new humanity which is to be glorified, as its exalted Lord is glorified..." (William F. Arndt and F. Wilbur Gingrich, *A Greek-English Lexicon of the New Testament and Other Early Christian Literature* [Chicago: The University of Chicago Press; Cambridge: at The University Press, 1960], p. 734). He is their chief and most excellent ruler.

The Messiah is preeminently the "Firstborn" (Ps. 89:28); and Israel was God's firstborn (Exodus 19:6); a "kingdom of priests" to God (Revelation 1:6); and therefore, the believer becomes part of God's "church of the firstborn" in Hebrews 12:23 (Jamieson, Fausset, and Brown, *op. cit.*, VI, 576). Radford writes that it is a description of the communion of the saints, living and departed, all alike eldest sons in a family where there is historical succession from generation to generation of the faithful, but no priority of spiritual status as between generations or within any generation (Lewis B. Radford, *The Epistles to the Colossians and the Epistle to Philemon* [London: Mouthen and Co., LTD, 1931], p. 168).

Pink would say the title, "Church of the Firstborn," is synonymous with the "...appointed heirs of all things..." (Hebrews 1:2) (Pink, *op cit.*, p. 53).

In Hebrews 1:6 we have a clear example of Christ's superiority, excellency and dignity, where the writer to the Hebrews tells us that God referred to Christ as His firstborn. And because Christ is superior to angels, they shall do obeisance to Him: "...And let all the angels of God worship him."

In Revelation 1:5 and Colossians 1:8, Christ is referred to as the "firstborn from the dead." It is obvious that the literal sense of the word cannot be used here. Also it cannot be used as the first to be raised from the dead. It can only mean preeminence or sovereignty, in that Christ was the first to be raised from the dead by His own power and to be exalted to immortality (John Gill, *An Exposition of the New Testament, both Doctrinal and Practical* [London: George Keith, 1876], IV, 382.), as the context in both cases corroborates. He is the "one to whom the bodies of His saints shall be conformed—see Philippians 3:21" (Pink, *loc. cit*). Both of these verses will be discussed in more detail.

In all these uses the employment of "firstborn" belongs to the Lord Jesus Christ, both as to the superiority of His nature, of His office and of His glory.

Church fathers gave strict attention to the fact that the Apostle Paul wrote πρωτοτοκος (first-born) and not πρωτοκτιοτι (first-created).

It is evident that there is a great contrast between the ideas of "birth" and "creation." They are not equivalent terms. Christ was "born" and the universe was "created." Meyer writes that the term πρωτοτκος is chosen, because...

in the comparison as to time of origin, it points to the peculiar *nature* of the origination in the case of *Christ,* namely, that He was not *created* by God, like the other beings in whom this is implied in the designation *ktisis*, but *born*, having come forth homogeneous from the nature of God. (H. A. W. Meyer, *Critical and Exegetical Handbook to the Epistles to the Philippians and Colossians and to Philemon* [New York: Funk and Wagnalls Publishers, 1885], p. 226.)

C. S. Lewis gives one of the best explanations of the difference between the concept of begetting and creating:

> One of the creeds says that Christ is the Son of God "begotten, not created"; and it adds "begotten by His Father before all worlds." Will you please get it quite clear that this has nothing to do with the fact that when Christ was born as a man on earth, that man was the son of a virgin? We are now thinking about something that happened before Nature was created at all, before time began. What does it mean?
>
> We don't use the words *begetting* or *begotten* much in modern English, but everyone still knows what they mean. To beget is to become the father of; to create.

Jesus Christ, the "firstborn," is before all creation in time, but not a part of creation.

The above discussion illustrates that the concept of priority is significant in the interpretation of "firstborn." But it is used in a secondary sense as will be seen below.

Lordship over (sovereignty). This meaning in the Old Testament often overshadowed and sometimes excludes the root meaning of priority in time. Moulton has determined that...

> when the Jew thought of a firstborn son his emphasis was not so much on the date of his birth as on his priority in the family and the privileges that were his by right. Paul's thought may be partly that Jesus is before us in time, but probably much more on the fact that He is supreme in rank above all the created world (Harold M. Moulton, *Colossians, Philippians, and Ephesians* [Epworth Preacher's Commentaries. London: The Epworth Press, 1963], p. 16).

God's firstborn is, "the natural ruler, the acknowledged head, of God's household." (Lightfoot, *Colossians*, p. 147.) The right of the firstborn is closely related to Messiah over all the created world. The phrase in Psalms 89:27, "...I will make him my firstborn," is explained by the addition of the "higher than the kings of the earth," speaking of

Messianic sovereignty. This reference to the meaning of sovereignty so predominated references to the Messiah that here "firstborn of all creation" would mean "Sovereign Lord over all creation by virtue of primogeniture" (*Ibid.*, p. 146).

The phrase, "...whom he hath appointed heir of all things..." in Hebrews 1:2, definitely relates to the "....I will make him my firstborn..." in Psalm 89:27. The latter phrase of Hebrews 1:2, "by whom also he made the worlds," is an epitome of Colossians 1:15-17. The meaning of supremacy so dominated the title in some of its uses that it was, as seen above, even used as a title of God Himself.

The Jehovah's Witnesses, in trying to establish Christ as a created being, render the "firstborn of all creation" in 1:15 as a partitive genitive (the whole of which it is part). In doing this they ignore the Old and New Testament usage of the term. This view is grammatically permissible; however, "this interpretation is exegetically and historically impossible; for verses 16, 17 emphatically distinguish between 'him' and the 'all things' of creation" (L. J. Baggott, *A New Approach to Colossians* [London: A. R. Mowbray and Co., Limited, 1961], p. 58).

The Witnesses try to substantiate their doctrine of Christ being one of the creation by a deliberate insertion of a word for which there is no basis in the Greek text. A clear example occurs here in *The New World Translation of the Christian Greek Scriptures*, Colossians 1:16, 17, which is pertinent to this discussion.

> ...because by means of him all [other] things were created in the heavens and upon the earth, the things visible and the things invisible, no matter whether they are thrones or lordships or governments or authorities. All [other] things have been created through him and for him. Also, he is before all [other] things and by means of him all other things were made to exist....

The word "other" has been inserted all the way through the passage unjustly. There is no equivalent word in the Greek text and no reputable translation includes it (Ray C. Stedman, "The New World Translation of the Christian Greek Scriptures," *Our Hope*, 50:32, July, 1953). When it is considered that the Jehovah's Witnesses assume Jesus

Christ to be a created being, it is easy to understand why they insert "other." The Greek solely states, "He is before all things and by him all things hold together," which is interpreted logically by Stedman to plainly teach "...that Christ is the Creator of everything that has existence, material or immaterial, and therefore He cannot Himself be a creature" (*Ibid*).

However, when the word "other" is unwarrantably interjected four times, it alters the thought to imply that Christ was the author of all created things, with the exception of one, Himself, who the Watchtower Society says was created. A footnote in the *New World Translation* reads, "All other: as at Luke 13:2, 4 and elsewhere" (*New World Translation of the Holy Scriptures* [Brooklyn: Watchtower Bible and Tract Society, 1963] p. 3385).

The reference here to Luke 13:2, 4 corresponds to the Lord's question about the Galileans whom Pilate had killed, and the 18 men who were slain by the falling tower of Siloam. He asks, "Do you suppose that these Galileans were greater sinners than all *other* Galileans..." and, "Or do you suppose that those 18...were worse culprits than all [the other—NWT] men who live in Jerusalem?" (*New American Standard Bible New Testament* [La Habra: The Foundation Press for the Lockman Foundation, 1963], p. 125).

Stedman, in his article, "The New World Translation of the Christian Greek Scriptures," set forth clearly the reason for the inclusion of "other" here and its exclusion in Colossians 1:15-18:

> Now here, though the original has no word for "other," it is plainly implied in the context, for, of course, these dead men were being put in contrast with all their fellow-citizens. However, there is no such implication in Colossians 1:15-17 *unless one presupposes that Christ Himself was nothing but a creature.* But no translator has the right thus to presuppose on a doctrinal issue. If the text were simply rendered as it is, leaving out the inserted word "other," it would agree exactly with other New Testament passages that declare plainly that the Lord Jesus Christ is Creator of everything that has been created (Hebrews 1:10; John 1:3).
>
> Again it is evident that the translators have taken special care to make the text say what they suppose it ought to say

rather than to let it speak plainly for itself (Stedman, *op. cit.*, p. 33).

Hebrews 2:10, not Luke 13, is the true parallel of Colossians 1:16, 17. It speaks so distinctly of Christ's creating all things that the New World committee did not dare to insert "other," in the text: "....for whose sake all things are and through whom all things are..." (Hebrews 2:10). (New World Translation, *op. cit.*, p. 3432).

It was decided by Baggott that "the idea of the Son of God being *part of* creation was entirely foreign to Paul's mind (see 2:9; I Corinthians 8:6; Philippians 2:6-8), and also the thought of his day (Baggott, *loc. cit.*). The partitive genitive in which πρωτότοκος would be as one of the class referred to, "creation," is usually expressed in the plural number, but the Apostle does not here use the plural (John Eadie, *Commentary on the Epistle of Paul to the Colossians* [Grand Rapids: Zondervan Publishing House, 1957], p. 49).

The use of sovereign as the primary meaning of "firstborn" in Colossians 1:15 also has its confirmation in Paul's aggressive denunciation of the Colossian heresy.

Thus, in a brief but concise passage of Scripture, Paul makes plain to his readers that Jesus Christ existed before creation and therefore is sovereign over creation. This passage does not teach or even support the Witnesses' doctrine that Jesus Christ was the first created being.

Paul used language that was understood in the Colossians' nomenclature. He purposely chose "firstborn."

We describe Christ in relation to all creation because it best characterizes the dignity, preeminence and sovereignty that belongs to Him as Lord of all. Therefore, in light of the historical, literal and metaphorical meanings of πρωτότοκος, the Jehovah's Witnesses are unscriptural in the application of it to Christ as created.

Jesus Christ, as taught in Colossians 1:15-18, is prior to, distinct from and sovereign over the universe.

Holy Spirit

According to the Watchtower Society the Holy Spirit is not part of the Godhead. Both the personality and the deity of the Holy Spirit [defined as "the invisible active force of Almighty God which moves His servants to do His will" (*Let God Be True*, p. 108)] are denied. The personality of the Holy Spirit is consistently rejected throughout the New World Translation by not capitalizing the term "spirit" when referring to the Holy Spirit.

To promulgate this error they mistranslate such passages as Ephesians 4:30 ("also, do not be grieving God's holy spirit, with which you have been sealed for a day of releasing by ransom"), and John 14:26 ("But the helper, the holy spirit which the Father will send in my name, that one will teach you all things and bring back to your minds all the things I told you").

However, both of these verses teach the personality of the Holy Spirit. How can one grieve something impersonal? Or how can an "impersonal force" teach all things? Competent translations substitute "with which" in Ephesians 4:30 with "by whom" and have "whom the Father will send" and "he will teach you" in John 14:26 rather than the impersonal holy spirit of the Watchtower.

Salvation

In Watchtower theology, salvation is not regarded as a free gift from God based upon Jesus Christ's work on the cross. Rather, their literature stresses a salvation by works. Russell wrote, "They must be recovered from blindness as well as from death, that they, each for himself, may have a full chance to prove, by obedience or disobedience, their worthiness of life eternal" (Charles Taze Russell, *Studies in the Scriptures*, Vol. 1, p. 158).

Elsewhere they state: "All who by reason of faith in Jehovah God and in Christ Jesus dedicate themselves to do God's will and then faithfully carry out their dedication will be rewarded with everlasting life..." (*Let God Be True*, p. 298).

The Bible teaches we are saved by grace through faith alone. Man's good works can never contribute to his salvation. "For by grace you have been saved through faith; and that not of yourselves, it is the gift of God; not as a result of works, that no one should boast" (Ephesians 2:8, 9 NASB). "He saved us, not on the basis of deeds which we have done in righteousness, but according to His mercy" (Titus 3:5 NASB).

Everlasting Punishment

The Watchtower denies the existence of hell as a place of everlasting punishment for the wicked. They argue, "The doctrine of a burning hell where the wicked are tortured eternally after death cannot be true mainly for four reasons: (1) It is wholly unscriptural; (2) it is unreasonable; (3) it is contrary to God's love; and (4) it is repugnant to justice" (*Let God Be True*, p. 9).

In response to this we contend that the doctrine is absolutely scriptural: "....when the Lord Jesus shall be revealed from Heaven with His mighty angels in flaming fire, dealing out retribution to those who do not know God and to those who do not obey the gospel of our Lord Jesus. And these will pay the penalty of eternal destruction, away from the presence of the Lord and from the glory of His power" (2 Thessalonians 1:7-9).

Matthew 25:46 speaks of eternal punishment and eternal life in the same context. Eternal punishment lasts as long as eternal life: "And these will go away into eternal punishment, but the righteous into eternal life."

The doctrine of everlasting punishment is neither contrary to God's love nor justice, as the Watchtower claims. Jesus Christ has taken the sins of the world upon Himself and offers everlasting life to all who will receive the free gift of God. If people reject His offer then they must suffer the penalty for their own sins.

False Prophecies

"When Jesus said He would come again He did not mean He would return in the flesh visible to men on earth. He has given up that earthly life as a ransom and therefore, can not take such life back again... The good news today is that Christ Jesus has come again, that God's Kingdom by Him has been set up and is now ruling in heaven... all the evidence shows that Jesus took up His Kingdom power and began his reign from Heaven in the year 1914" (Pamphlet, "This Good News of the Kingdom", pp. 19, 21).

The idea that the second coming of Christ took place in

1914 is important to Watchtower theology. That was the time, they say, that God's kingdom was fully set up in heaven. However, this was not always their teaching. Before 1914, the Watchtower was predicting that God's Kingdom was to be set up on *earth* (not in heaven) in 1914!

"'The times of the Gentiles' extend to 1914. And the Heavenly Kingdom will not have full sway till then, but as a 'stone' the Kingdom of God is set up 'in the days of these Kings' and by consummating them it becomes a universal Kingdom — a 'great mountain and fills the whole earth'" (*Watchtower Reprints*, Vol. I, March, 1880, p. 82).

Charles Taze Russell also stated that the world would see "the full establishment of the Kingdom of God in the earth at A.D. 1914, the terminus of the times of the Gentiles" (C. T. Russell, *Thy Kingdom Come*, 1891, p. 126).

The prophecies made by Russell and the Watchtower concerning 1914 totally failed because the Kingdom of God was not established upon the earth. Today, as already observed, the Watchtower teaches that Christ returned invisibly in 1914 and set up His Kingdom only in Heaven. However, this idea clearly opposes the scriptural teaching of the visible bodily return of Christ: "Ye men of Galilee, why stand ye gazing up into heaven? This same Jesus which is taken up from you into heaven, shall so come in like manner as ye have seen Him go into Heaven" (Acts 1:11).

Jesus warned against such false teaching about His return: "Wherefore if they shall say unto you, Behold, he is in the desert; go not forth: Behold, he is in the secret chambers; believe it not. For as the lightning cometh out of the East, and shineth even unto the West; so shall the coming of the Son of Man be" (Matthew 24:26, 27). The Scriptures also state: "Behold, he cometh with the clouds; and every eye shall see Him..." (Revelation 1:7).

The Watchtower is guilty of false prophecy (Deuteronomy 18:21, 22) in wrongly predicting the date 1914 to be the return of Christ. They are also wrong in asserting His coming is secret and invisible because the Scriptures teach completely to the contrary (Revelation 1:7).

The New World Translation

In 1961, the Watchtower Bible and Tract Society published the *New World Translation of the Holy Scriptures.* The rationale for this new translation was given when the New Testament was published in 1950:

> But honesty compels us to remark that, while each of them (other translations) has its points of merit, they have fallen victim to the power of human traditionalism in varying degrees, consequently, religious traditions, hoary with age, have been taken for granted and gone unchallenged and uninvestigated. These have been interwoven into the translations to color the thought. In support of a preferred religious view, an inconsistency and unreasonableness have been insinuated into the teachings of the inspired writings.
>
> The Son of God taught that the traditions of creed-bound men made the commandments and teachings of God of no power and effect. The endeavor of the New World Bible Translation committee has been to avoid this snare of religious traditionalism. (Foreword to *New World Translation of the Christian Greek Scriptures,* 1961).

The translators of the New World Translation have not achieved their goal. Their work is a highly biased attempt to justify some of their non-biblical doctrines. In terms of scholarship, the New World Translation leaves much to be desired. The following examples will make the point clear.

John 1:1

One of the readings of the New World Translation that has caused considerable outrage among Greek scholars is its totally unsupportable rendering of the last clause of John 1:1, "The word was a god." This translation makes Jesus Christ less than God, relegating Him to the position of a "created being" in accordance with Watchtower theology. There is no basis whatsoever for this rendering, although the Watchtower would have people believe the contrary.

> "...How are we to understand John 1:1, 2 of which there are differing translations? Many translations read: 'And the Word was with God, and the Word was God.' Others read: 'And the Word (The Logos) was divine." Another: 'and the Word was God.' Others 'And the Word was a god.' Since we have

examined so much of what John wrote about Jesus who was the Word made flesh we are now in a position to determine which of those several translations is correct. It means our salvation" (*The Word Who Is He? According to John*, p. 52).

This is a misleading statement because it gives the impression that other translations agree with their rendering when the opposite is true. There are *no* reputable authorities or translations that support the reading, "The Word was a god."

The only other translation quoted in this Watchtower publication that reads the same way is *The New Testament in an Improved Version upon the Basis of Archbishop Newcome's New Translation: with a Corrected Text*, printed in London in 1808. Such an antiquated and obscure translation done by a Unitarian cannot be considered reputable.

Grammatical Explanation of John 1:1 The grammatical explanation given by the Watchtower for its translation of John 1:1 is unsatisfactory. They contend that when *theos* (the Greek word for God) appears in John 1:1 it appears twice, once with the definite article (the) and once without. When it appears without the definite article (in the last clause of John 1:1) they feel justified in translating it, "And the Word was a god...."

"Careful translators recognize that the articular construction of the noun [with the definite article] points to an identity, a personality, whereas an anarthrous construction (without the definite article) points to a quality about someone" (Appendix to the *Kingdom Interlinear Translation of the Greek Scriptures*, Watchtower Bible and Tract Society, p. 1158).

Not only is the above statement incorrect, it is also inconsistently applied throughout the Watchtower's own translation. In the first 18 verses of John's gospel, the word for God—*theos*—appears six times without the definite article (vs. 1, 6, 12, 13, and twice in 18). Yet, it is rendered God (referring to Jehovah) in each instance except for the last clause of verse one when it refers to Jesus!

If the Watchtower's translations were consistent, verse six should read, "There arose a man that was sent forth as a representative of a god." Moreover, verse 12 should read "to become a god's children," etc. Why only in verse one do they refuse to translate *theos* as God (meaning Jehovah)?

We conclude that there is no basis for translating John 1:1, "The Word was a god" as in the *New World Translation*. It is a biased rendering that cannot be justified grammatically.

They do not want to acknowledge what is clearly taught in verse one: Jesus Christ is God. Also, it should be observed that the absence of the definite article does *not* indicate someone other than the true God. The entry on *theos* in the authoritative *Arndt and Gingrich Greek Lexicon* states *theos* is used "quite predominately of the true God, sometimes with, sometimes without, the article" (William F. Arndt and F. Wilbur Gingrich, *Greek-English Lexicon of the New Testament*, 1957, p. 357).

(Further information on the Greek construction and translation of John 1:1 has been presented by many other writers in complete form. See the recommended reading list for works that deal extensively with Jehovah's Witnesses. Suffice it to say, the Watchtower mistranslation of John 1:1 is not supported by any contextual grammatical study.)

Even without going to the Greek grammar of John 1:1, we can see that the Watchtower translation of John 1:1 goes against the clear teachings of the Bible. In both the Old and New Testaments we are taught that there is only one true God (Isaiah 43:10; John 17:3; 1 Corinthians 8:4-6, etc.). All other "gods" are false gods. Those who would acknowledge any god as true except for Jehovah God are guilty of breaking the first commandment: "You shall have no other gods before me" (Exodus 20:3).

By translating the last part of John 1:1 as, "The Word was a god," the Watchtower has declared its belief in polytheism, or the belief in more than one god. According to the whole testimony of the Bible, the Word (Jesus Christ) of John 1:1 must be either the only true God, Jehovah, or a false god. The Bible knows only one true God, Jehovah.

Jehovah's Witnesses will not call Jesus Christ a false god. Neither will they call him Jehovah, the one true God. By calling Jesus Christ "a god" in John 1:1, they have acknowledged their own polytheism, which is contrary to the Bible, the Word of God.

John 8:58

In the eighth chapter of the gospel of John, Jesus is asked by the religious leaders, "Whom do you make yourself out to be?" (verse 53). He answered, "Before Abraham was, I Am" (verse 58). His answer is a direct reference to Exodus 3:14 where God identifies Himself from the burning bush to Moses by the designation, "I Am." The Jews, realizing that Jesus claimed to be God, attempted to stone Him for blashemy (verse 59).

The *New World Translation* mistranslates this verse by making it read, "Before Abraham came into existence I have been." The footnote to John 8:58 in the 1950 edition is enlightening: "I have been — 'ego eimi' after the aorist infinitive clause and hence properly rendered in the perfect indefinite tense. It is not the same as 'Ho ohn' meaning 'The Being' or 'the I AM' at Exodus 3:14 LXX" (*New World Translation*, 1950, p. 312).

This is not in any "perfect indefinite tense." The Watchtower then changed the note to read "the perfect tense," dropping the word *indefinite* (see *The Kingdom Interlinear Translation of the Greek Scriptures*, 1969). However, this is also incorrect since the verb *eimi* is in the present tense, indicative mood, and hence should properly be translated, "I Am." Moreover, the context of John 8:58 (8:42 – 9:12), the verb "to be" occurs 22 times in the indicative mood and the *New World Translation* correctly renders 21 out of 22. The only incorrect rendering is in John 8:58. Why?

Furthermore, the footnote is deliberately misleading. The Septuagint (abbreviated as LXX), the Greek translation of the Hebrew Old Testament, translated the name of God in Exodus 3:14 with the Greek *Ego Eimi ho ohn* (I am The Being). The Watchtower's note obscures the correlation between the two passages by failing to cite *ego eimi* as part of the Septuagint translation. Their note reads, "It is not the same as *ho ohn*, meaning 'the being' or 'The I Am' at Exodus 3:14, LXX."

While the Hebrew text repeats the same form of the "to be" verb in Exodus 3:14, customary Greek usage makes it more natural for the Greek translation of Exodus 3:14 to first express the term as *ego eimi* (I am) and then a different variation of the same term, *ho ohn* (the Being). In conclusion, the Watchtower has blatantly misrepresented the Greek argument for Christ's deity from John 8:58. Jesus Christ is clearly identifying Himself as the *Ego eimi (ho ohn)* of Exodus 3:14.

Dr. A. T. Robertson, one of the greatest Greek scholars who ever lived, after translating *"ego eimi"* as "I AM," had this to say about John 8:58: "Undoubtedly here Jesus claims eternal existence with the absolute phrase used of God" (*Word Pictures in the New Testament*, Vol. V, pp. 158-159).

The Watchtower betrays itself in its own *Kingdom Interlinear Translation* which contains a literal English translation beneath the Greek text as well as the New World Translation reading. In John 8:58 under the Greek *ego eimi*, *The Kingdom Interlinear* rightly translates it, "I am", but *New World Translation* changes it to, "I have been." This inconsistency is striking.

There is no sufficient basis for the translation, "I have been," in John 8:58. This is another example of the scholarly shortcomings of the Watchtower. It obscures the fact that Jesus Christ is Jehovah God.

Colossians 1

In Colossians one, the Apostle Paul stresses the Lordship and deity of Jesus Christ by emphasizing that He is the creator of all things: "For by Him all things were created" (1:16). However, the *New World Translation*, with absolutely no legitimate justification, adds the word "other" in this verse and five other places in chapter one in an attempt to make Jesus a created being:

Vs. 16, Because by means of Him all [other] things were created in the Heavens and upon the earth (NWT).

Vs. 16, All [other] things have been created through Him and for Him (NWT).

Vs. 17, Also, He is before all [other] things and by means of Him all [other] things were made to exist (NWT).

Vs. 20, And through Him to reconcile again to Himself all [other] things (NWT).

There is no basis for adding the word "other" to the texts listed above. On the contrary, to do so destroys the natural context of the passages and improperly implies that Jesus Christ is Himself a creature. Since Jehovah God alone created all things (Isaiah 44:24; Hebrews 3:4), and

Colossians calls Jesus Christ the creator, we can justifiably assume that Jesus Christ is Jehovah God.

We conclude, *The New World Translation* is not a work of competent scholarship, but rather an attempt to promulgate the doctrines of the Watchtower. The foreword of the New World Translation states, "It is a very responsible thing to translate the Holy Scriptures from their original languages." We agree wholeheartedly and we wish the Watchtower had lived up to this high principle.

Conclusion

A close examination of the Watchtower has demonstrated that it is not what it claims to be: the "sole collective channel for the flow of biblical truth." It is guilty of false prophecy, anti-biblical theology, and misrepresentation of the truth.

We heartily recommend to Jehovah's Witnesses that they act on the following instruction from the Watchtower: "We need to examine, not only what we personally believe, but also what is taught by any religious organization with which we may be associated. Are its teachings in full harmony with God's Word, or are they based on the traditions of men? If we are lovers of the Truth, there is nothing to fear from such an examination" (*The Truth That Leads to Eternal Life*, 1968, p. 13).

Such an examination will show the shortcomings of the man-made Watchtower and the all-sufficient perfection of Jesus Christ, our "great God and Saviour" (Titus 2:13).

Jehovah's Witnesses Terms

Annihilation—According to the Jehovah's Witnesses, unbelievers will not receive eternal punishment but rather will be annihilated, or cease to exist.

Arius—A heretic who lived in the fourth century A.D. who denied the fact that Jesus Christ was eternal God. His arguments against the deity of Christ have been repeated by such groups as Jehovah's Witnesses and the Unitarians.

Christadelphians—Cult founded in 1848 by John Thomas. It teaches among other unbiblical doctrines that Jesus Christ is not God and that the Holy Spirit is only a power, a forerunner of Jehovah's Witnesses.

Franz, Frederick W. — Fourth and current president of the Watchtower Bible and Tract Society.

Little Flock — Another designation for the 144,000 Jehovah's Witnesses who live in heaven after their death. All other Jehovah's Witnesses are barred from heaven and live instead on Paradise Earth.

Michael the Archangel — According to the Watchtower, Jehovah's first creation, the archangel who later became the man Jesus.

Nathan Knorr — Third president of the Watchtower Bible and Tract Society. During his leadership (1942-1977) the Society increased from 115,000 to over two million members.

New World Translation of the Holy Scriptures — The official translation of the Bible by the Jehovah's Witnesses, characterized by their own biased interpretations.

Russell, Charles Taze — The founder of what is the present-day Jehovah's Witnesses (Watchtower Bible and Tract Society). Russell wrote voluminously including the six-volume work, *Studies in the Scriptures*, where he expounded his aberrational doctrines.

Rutherford, Judge J. F. — Second president of the Watchtower Bible and Tract Society. Gave group the name Jehovah's Witnesses in 1931. Rutherford centralized the authority of the Witnesses during his reign to its present-day headquarters in Brooklyn, New York.

Studies in the Scriptures — Seven-volume work, six of which were written by Charles Taze Russell, founder of Jehovah's Witnesses, that expounds the basic teachings of the Jehovah's Witnesses.

The Awake — Watchtower periodical designed to evangelize the public.

The Harp of God — A book by Judge Joseph Rutherford, second president of Jehovah's Witnesses, explaining Watchtower theology.

The Truth That Leads to Everlasting Life — Watchtower study book designed to introduce one to the Watchtower teachings.

The Watchtower — One of the official publications of the Jehovah's Witnesses.

CHAPTER SIX

Mormonism

"**B**ut even though we, or an angel from heaven, should preach to you a gospel contrary to that which we have preached to you, let him be accursed" (Galatians 1:8 NASB).

History

The founder of Mormonism, or The Church of Jesus Christ of Latter-Day Saints, Joseph Smith, Jr., was born on December 23, 1805 in Sharon, Vermont. Smith was the fourth of ten children of Joseph and Lucy Mack Smith. In 1817 the family moved to Palmyra, New York (near present-day Rochester).

Most of the members of the Smith family soon joined the Presbyterian church, but young Joseph remained undecided. His argument was that all the strife and tension among the various denominations made him question which denomination was right. It was this conflict that set the stage for Joseph's alleged first vision.

The First Vision

In 1820 Joseph allegedly received a vision that became the basis for the founding of the Mormon Church. According to Mormon history, the background of Joseph's first vision was a revival that broke out in the spring of 1820, in Palmyra, New York:

Indeed, the whole district of the country seemed affected by it, and great multitudes united themselves to the different religious parties, which created no small stir and division amongst the people, some crying, "Lo, here!" and others, "Lo, there!" Some were contending for the Methodist faith, some for the Presbyterian and some for the Baptist (Joseph Smith, *The Pearl of Great Price*, 2:5).

This led to Joseph's inquiry of the Lord as to which of these denominations was right. Smith reported the incident as follows:

My object in going to inquire of the Lord was to know which of all the sects was right, that I might know which to join. No sooner, therefore, did I get possession of myself, so as to be able to speak, than I asked the personages who stood above me in the light, which of all the sects was right—and which I should join.

I was answered that I must join none of them, for they were all wrong; and the personage who addressed me said that all their creeds were an abomination in His sight; that those professors were all corrupt; that: "they draw near to me with their lips, but their hearts are far from me, they teach for doctrines the commandments of men, having a form of godliness, but they deny the power thereof" (Joseph Smith, *The Pearl of Great Price*, 2:18, 19).

The Second Vision

Joseph then recounts a second vision he had on September 21, 1823, in which he claims:

I had a second vision. A personage appeared at my bedside who was glorious beyond description. He said that he was a messenger sent from the Presence of God, and that his name was Moroni; that God had a work for me to do, and that my name should be had for good and evil among all nations, kindreds and tongues.

He told me that a book had been deposited, written on golden plates, giving an account of the former inhabitants of this continent and containing "the fullness of the everlasting Gospel" as delivered by the saviour to the ancient inhabitants of this land. He also said that there were two stones in silver bows—and these stones, fastened to a breastplate, constituted what is called the Urim and Thummin—deposited with the plates, adding that God had prepared these stones for the purpose of translating this book.

I was shown exactly where the plates had been deposited.

That same night the heavenly messenger appeared again twice, each time repeating the same message. The next day I went to a hill outside the village where we lived (now called the Hill Cumorah) and found the golden plate deposited in a stone box with the Urim and Thummin and the breastplate.

I was not permitted to take them out at this time, however, but was told by the angel, who had reappeared, that I should come back to this place every year at this time for the next four years. Finally, however, on September 22, 1827, I was given the plates by the heavenly messenger with the instructions to keep them carefully until he, the angel, should call for them again (*The Pearl of Great Price*, pp. 50-54).

Obeying the Heavenly Messenger

Joseph then moved to his father-in-law's house in Harmony, Pennsylvania where, with supposedly divine help, he began to copy the characters off the plates and translate them. The publication of the translation of the plates was financed by a New York farmer named Martin Harris who was told by Smith that the writing on the plates was "reformed Egyptian." The translation was finally completed and placed on sale on March 26, 1830.

A little over a week later, on April 6, 1830, at Fayette, New York, "the church of Christ" was officially organized with six members. The name was eventually changed to the Church of Jesus Christ of Latter-Day Saints. The number of members increased rapidly and a group of them moved to Kirtland, Ohio (near present-day Cleveland). It was here that Joseph supervised the first printing of the divine revelations he had received.

First known as the *Book of Commandments*, the work has undergone significant and numerous changes and now constitutes one of the Mormon sacred works, retitled *Doctrine and Covenants*. Smith also worked on a revision ("divinely aided") of the King James Version of the Bible.

Although the Mormon church began to grow in numbers while expanding westward, it was not without persecution. Battles were fought between Mormons and their non-Mormon counterparts in Far West, Missouri, a town founded by the Mormons. Here Smith was imprisoned along with some other Mormon leaders.

After escaping, he and his followers moved to Illinois to a town Smith named Nauvoo, where he organized a small army and gave himself the title of Lieutenant-General. During this time, the Mormons were busily constructing a temple and evangelizing the populace.

When a local paper, the *Nauvoo Expositor*, began publishing anti-Mormon material, Smith ordered the press destroyed and every copy of the paper burned. This act led to Smith's arrest and imprisonment. Released and then rearrested, Smith was taken to jail in Carthage, Illinois along with his brother Hyrum.

On June 27, 1844, a mob of about 200 people, their faces blackened to avoid recognition, stormed the jail and shot and killed Joseph and Hyrum Smith. Joseph did not die without a fight. According to the church's own account he shot several of the mob members with a gun he had (see *History of the Church*, 6:617-18). The Mormons, however, considered Joseph Smith a martyr for the cause.

Brigham Young

After the death of Joseph Smith the leadership went to Brigham Young, the President of the Twelve Apostles, who convinced the great majority of Mormons that he was their rightful successor.

Young led the group westward in a journey which saw many hardships including Indian attacks, exposure and internal strife. On July 24, 1847, they arrived at Salt Lake Valley in Utah which became the headquarters of the Mormon church. By the time of Young's death in 1877, the members numbered approximately 150,000. Today, the church has over four million members worldwide.

The Claims of Mormonism

The Mormons claim they are the restoration of the true church established by Jesus Christ. It is not Protestant or Catholic, but claims, rather, to be the only true church. "If it had not been for Joseph Smith and the restoration, there would be no salvation outside the Church of Jesus Christ of Latter-Day Saints" (Bruce R. McConkie, *Mormon Doctrine*, p. 670).

"No salvation without accepting Joseph Smith...If Joseph Smith was verily a prophet, and if he told the truth...then this knowledge is of the most vital importance to the entire world. No man can reject that testimony without incurring the most dreadful consequences, for he can not enter the Kingdom of God" (Joseph Fielding Smith, *Doctrines of Salvation*, pp. 189-190).

The claims of Joseph Smith and his followers are clear. The Church of Jesus Christ of Latter-Day Saints claims it is God's true church on earth while all the others are wrong. Commenting on Joseph Smith's first vision, Dr. Walter Martin puts the matter into perspective:

> With one "Special Revelation" the Mormon Church expects its intended converts to accept the totally unsupported testimony of a fifteen-year-old boy that nobody ever preached Jesus Christ's gospel from the close of the Apostolic age until the "Restoration" through Joseph Smith, Jr., beginning in 1820! We are asked to believe that the Church Fathers for the first five centuries did not proclaim the true gospel—that Origen, Justin, Iraneaus, Jerome, Eusebius, Athanasius, Chrysostom, and then later Thomas Aquinas, Huss, Luther, Calvin, Zwingli, Tyndale, Wycliffe, Knox, Wesley, Whitefield, and a vast army of faithful servants of Jesus Christ all failed where Joseph Smith Jr., was to succeed!
>
> With one dogmatic assertion, Joseph pronounced everybody wrong, all Christian theology an abomination, and all professing Christians corrupt—all in the name of God! How strange for this to be presented as restored Christianity, when Jesus Christ specifically promised that "the gates of Hell" would not prevail against the church (Matthew 16:18)! In Mormonism we find God contradicting this statement in a vision to Joseph Smith Jr., some 18 centuries later! (*The Maze of Mormonism*, 1978, p. 31).

The Mormons make the claim that they are the "restored church of Jesus Christ" but the facts totally discount their claim.

Sources of Authority

The Mormon Church has four accepted sacred works: the Bible, the *Book of Mormon*, *Doctrine and Covenants*, and *The Pearl of Great Price*. The present prophet's words are also a source of authority.

The Bible

The Mormon articles of faith read, "We believe the Bible to be the Word of God in so far as it is translated correctly..." (*Articles of Faith of the Church of Jesus Christ of Latter-Day Saints*, Article 8). The Book of Mormon claims that a correct translation of the Bible is impossible since the Catholic Church has taken away from the word of God "...many parts which are plain and most precious; and also many covenants of the Lord have they taken away. And all this have they taken away. And all this have they done that they might pervert the right ways of the Lord" (1 Nephi 13:26b, 27).

Orson Pratt, an early apostle of the Mormon Church, put it this way, "Who knows that even one verse of the Bible has escaped pollution, so as to convey the same sense now that it did in the original?" (*Orson Pratt's Works*, 1891, p. 218).

Thus the Mormons put more trust in the other three sacred books, which have escaped pollution, than they do in the Bible. This opens the door for the Mormons to add their new non-biblical teachings by claiming they were doctrines deliberately removed by the Catholic Church. The claim that the Scriptures have been changed and corrupted throughout the centuries is totally false (see *Answers*, Here's Life Publishers, 1980, pp. 4-6).

The Book of Mormon

The *Book of Mormon* is also considered inspired: "We also believe the Book of Mormon to be the Word of God" (*Articles of Faith*, Section Eight). The *Book of Mormon* is supposedly an account of the original inhabitants of America to whom Christ appeared after His resurrection.

Doctrine and Covenants

Doctrine and Covenants is a record of 136 revelations revealing some of Mormonism's distinctive doctrines such as baptism for the dead and celestial marriage.

The Pearl of Great Price

The *Pearl of Great Price* contains the *Book of Moses*, which is roughly equivalent to the first six chapters of Genesis, and *The Book of Abraham*, a translation of an Egyptian Papyrus that later proved to be fraudulent. It also contains an extract from Joseph Smith's translation of the

Bible; extracts from the *History of Joseph Smith*, which is his autobiography; and the *Articles of Faith*.

The Living Prophets

The living prophet also occupies an important part in present-day Mormonism. Ezra Taft Benson, who at the time of this writing is President of the Council of the Twelve Apostles, said in a speech on February 26, 1980, at Brigham Young University, that the living prophet (head of the church) is "more vital to us than the standard works." This echoed what was given to the ward teachers (similar to Christian Education adult teachers) in 1945.

> Any Latter-day Saint who denounces or opposes, whether actively or otherwise, any plan or doctrine advocated by the prophets, seers, and revelators of the Church is cultivating the spirit of apostasy...Lucifer...wins a great victory when he can get members of the Church to speak against their leaders and to do their own thinking...
>
> "When our leaders speak, the thinking has been done. When they propose a plan—it is God's plan. When they point the way, there is no other which is safe. When they give directions, it should mark the end of the controversy (*Improvement Era*, June 1945, p. 354).

The Bible Says

The Bible contradicts the Mormon reliance on multiple contradictory revelations. While the Mormon scriptures contradict each other and the Bible, the Bible never contradicts itself and the God of the Bible never contradicts Himself. Hebrews 1:1-3 tells us what the source of our knowledge of God comes from:

> God, after He spoke long ago to the fathers in the prophets in many portions and in many ways, in these last days has spoken to us in His Son, whom He appointed heir of all things, through whom also He made the world. And He is the radiance of His glory and the exact representation of His nature, and upholds all things by the word of His power. When He had made purification of sins, He sat down at the right hand of the Majesty on high...

Any message that purports to be from God must agree with the message already brought by Jesus Christ in fulfillment of the Old Testament (Luke 24:27). Eternal life comes from the works and gift of Jesus Christ, not from Joseph Smith, Brigham Young, or any other false Mormon prophet (John 20:31). Proverbs 30:5, 6 warns those who try to add to God's Word, saying, "Every word of God is tested; He is a shield to those who take refuge in Him. Do not add to His words lest He reprove you, and you be proved a liar."

The Mormon Doctrine of God

"We believe in God, the Eternal Father, and His Son Jesus Christ, and in the Holy Ghost" (Joseph Smith, *The Pearl of Great Price*, Articles of Faith, p. 59).

The above statement leaves the impression that Mormons believe the biblical doctrine of the Holy Trinity—namely, there is one God who manifests himself in three persons, the Father, the Son, and the Holy Spirit, and these three persons are the one God. However, nothing could be further from the truth.

The Mormon doctrine of God is contradictory to what the Bible teaches. The Mormons believe in many gods and teach that God himself was once a man. Moreover, Mormon males have the possibility of attaining godhood. Joseph Smith made this clear in *The King Follett Discourse:*

> I am going to inquire after God: for I want you all to know him and be familiar with him...I will go back to the beginning before the world was, to show you what kind of a being God is.
>
> God was once as we are now, and is an exalted man, and sits enthroned in yonder heavens...I say, if you were to see him today, you would see him like a man in a form like yourselves in all the person, image, and very form of a man.
>
> I am going to tell you how God came to be God. We have imagined and supposed that God was God from all eternity. I will refute that idea and take away the veil so that you may see.
>
> It is the first principle of the gospel to know for certainty the character of God and to know that we may converse with him as one man with another, and that he was once a man like us; yea, that God himself, the father of us all, dwelt on an earth, the same as Jesus Christ did.
>
> Here then, is eternal life—to know the only wise and true God; and you have got to learn how to be Gods yourselves,

and to be kings and priests to God, the same as all Gods have done before you (Joseph Smith Jr., *King Follett Discourse*, pp. 8-10).

Other statements by Smith and Young reveal further the Mormon concept of God:

> In the beginning, the head of the Gods called a council of the Gods; and they came together and concocted a plan to create and populate the world and people it (Joseph Smith, *Journal of Discourses*, 6:5).
>
> The Father has a body of flesh and bones as tangible as man's (Joseph Smith, *Doctrine and Covenants*, 130:22).

Lorenzo Snow repeated Joseph Smith's words about the Mormon idea of God,

> As Man is, God was,
>> As God, is, Man may become.
>
> (Joseph Smith, *King Follett Discourse*, p. 9, note by Lorenzo Smith).

The Mormon writer Milton Hunter came to the obvious conclusion:

> Mormon prophets have continuously taught the sublime truth that God the Eternal Father was once a mortal man who passed through a school earth similar to that through which we are passing. He became God—an exalted being (Milton R. Hunter, *The Gospel Through the Ages*, p. 104).

Smith's teaching on the nature of God not only contradicts the Bible, it also contradicts the Book of Mormon!

> And Zeezrom said unto him: 'Thou sayest that there is a true and living God?' And Amulek said: 'Yea, there is a true and living God.' Now Zeezrom said: 'Is there more than one God?' And he answered, 'No!' (Alma 11:26-29).

See also Alma 11:21, 22; 2 Nephi 11:7; 2 Nephi 31:21; 3 Nephi 11:27, 36; Mosiah 15:1-5, Mosiah 16:15.

The Bible repeatedly affirms that there is only one true God. Isaiah 43:10 emphatically declares, "You are My witnesses, declares the Lord, and My servant whom I have chosen, in order that you may know and believe Me, and understand that I am He. Before Me there was no God formed, and there will be none after Me."

In the New Testament we are assured that though there are false gods and idols worshipped by men, they are worthless. "...we know there is no such thing as an idol in the world, and that there is no God but one" (1 Corinthians 8:4).

Jesus Christ

The Mormon Church teaches that Jesus Christ was a preexistent spirit like the rest of us. Even though we are all literally brothers and sisters of Jesus, He is set apart from the rest of us by being the firstborn of God's spirit-children. "And now, verily I say unto you, I was in the beginning with the Father, and am the Firstborn; and all those who are begotten through me are partakers of the glory of the same, and are the church of the Firstborn. Ye were also in the beginning with the Father" (*Doctrine and Covenants* 93:21-23).

In Mormonism Jesus is not the unique Son of God:

> His humanity is to be recognized as real and ordinary— whatever happened to Him may happen to any one of us. The Divinity of Jesus and the Divinity of all other noble and stately souls, in so far as they, too, have been influenced by a spark of Deity—can be recognized as manifestations of the Divine (Elder B. H. Roberts citing Sir Oliver Lodge in Joseph Smith, *King Follett Discourse*, p. 11 note).

Man

According to Mormonism, man is a preexistent soul who takes his body at birth in this world.

> Man is a spirit clothed with a tabernacle. The intelligent part of which was never created or made, but existed eternally— man was also in the beginning with God (Joseph Fielding Smith, *Progess of Man*).

> Speaking of man, John Widtsoe said, "He existed before he came to earth: He was with God 'in the beginning.' Man's destiny is divine. Man is an eternal being. He also is 'everlasting to everlasting'" (*Varieties of American Religion*, p. 132).

Contrary to Mormon theology, Jesus Christ is the unique Son of God. John 1:14 declares that He "became flesh, and dwelt among us, and we beheld His glory, glory as of the only begotten from the Father, full of grace and truth." Jesus Christ reflected the power of God while on earth that no other man could ever achieve: "He is the

image of the invisible God, the firstborn of all creation"
(Colossians 1:15). To think that we can one day be God
like Jesus Christ and the Father is blasphemous. There is
an eternal chasm between the Creator and the created.
The Bible soundly condemns those who would think
otherwise:

> Professing to be wise, they became fools, and exchanged the
> glory of the incorruptible God for an image in the form of
> corruptible man and of birds and four-footed animals and
> crawling creatures. Therefore God gave them over in the
> lusts of their hearts to impurity, that their bodies might be
> dishonored among them. For they exchanged the truth of God
> for a lie, and worshipped and served the creature rather than
> the Creator, who is blessed forever. Amen (Romans 1:22-25).

Salvation

Articles 2 and 3 of the *Mormon Articles of Faith* spell
out their doctrine of salvation:

> No. 2: "We believe that men shall be punished for their own
> sins and not for Adam's transgression."
> No. 3: "We believe that through the atonement of Christ,
> all mankind may be saved, by obedience to the laws and
> ordinances of the Gospel."

James Talmage in his work *Articles of Faith* explains
what this means:

> The extent of the Atonement is universal, applying alike to
> all descendants of Adam. Even the unbeliever, the heathen
> and the child who dies before reaching the years of discretion
> all are redeemed by the Saviour's self-sacrifice from the in-
> dividual consequences of the fall...of the saved not all will
> be exalted to the higher glories. No one can be admitted to
> any order of glory, in short, no soul can be saved until Justice
> has been satisfied for violated law...In the kingdom of God
> there are numerous levels of gradations provided for those
> who are worthy of them (James Talmage, *Articles of Faith*,
> pp. 85, 91).

Thus in Mormonism there is a general salvation for all
mankind and an individual salvation for each person.
There is, to the Mormon, no such thing as hell or
everlasting punishment. Everyone will eventually go to
one of the three levels of glory: the celestial kingdom
which is reserved for the Melchizedek priesthood

members who will become gods; the terrestial kingdom, for those who failed the requirements of exaltation; and lastly, the telestial kingdom, for those who have no testimony of Christ.

> I want you to tell them and tell all the great men of the earth, that the Latter-day Saints are to be their redeemer... Believe in God, believe in Jesus, and believe in Joseph his prophet, and Brigham his successor, and I add, If you will believe in your hearts and confess with your mouth Jesus is the Christ, that Joseph was a prophet, and that Brigham is his successor, you shall be saved in the kingdom of God...
>
> No man or woman in this dispensation will ever enter into the Celestial Kingdom of God without the consent of Joseph Smith... every man and woman must have the certificate of Joseph Smith, Junior, as a passport to their entrance into the mansions where God and Christ are—I can not go there without his consent... He reigns there as supreme, a being in his sphere, capacity, calling, as God does in Heaven (Brigham Young, *Journal of Discourses*, 6:299, 7:289).

Salvation according to the Bible is a free gift from Jesus Christ our Lord. Ephesians 2:8-10 declares, "For by grace you have been saved through faith; and that not of yourselves, it is the gift of God; not as a result of works, that no one should boast. For we are His workmanship, created in Christ Jesus for good works, which God prepared beforehand, that we should walk in them."

When the people asked Jesus, "What shall we do, that we may work the works of God?" (John 6:28), Jesus replied, "This is the work of God, that you believe in Him whom He has sent" (v. 29). There is no way to earn salvation. One's good works are testimony to the accomplished fact of one's salvation, purchased not by works, but by the blood of Jesus Christ. We are saved through Christ's sacrifice on the cross for our sins, not because of anything we can do ourselves. Hebrews 7:27 says that when Jesus offered Himself for man's sin it was "once for all."

Changes in the Book of Mormon

The *Book of Mormon* according to Joseph Smith, Jr., is "the most correct of any book on earth" (Joseph Smith, Jr., *History of the Church*, 4:461). However, this "most" correct book has, from the 1830 edition to the modern edition, undergone some 3,000 changes.

> And after having received the record of the Nephites, yea even my servant Joseph Smith, Jr., might have power to translate through the mercy of God, by the power of God, the Book of Mormon (*Doctrine and Covenants*, Section 1, verse 29).

> And gave him (Joseph Smith, Jr.) power from on high, by the means which were before prepared, to translate the Book of Mormon (*Doctrine and Covenants*, Section 20, verse 8).

The two quotations from the *Doctrine and Covenants*, according to Mormon belief, are revelations given through Joseph Smith, Jr., from the Lord, and they confirm the authenticity and genuineness of the *Book of Mormon*. The first quotation is from a revelation dated November 1, 1831, well over a year after the *Book of Mormon* was published in early 1830.

The revelations claim the *Book of Mormon* was translated by the power of God, that Joseph Smith was a servant used of God to translate the *Book of Mormon* using means that God had prepared for translating and that well over a year after its publication, the Lord affirmed the authenticity of the *Book of Mormon*. Yet a comparison of the latest edition with the first edition (the 1830 edition that was supposed to be translated by the power of God) will show the more than 3,000 changes.

Original (1830) Edition	Modern Version
...King Benjamin had a gift from God, whereby he could interpret such engravings ...(p. 200)	...King Mosiah had a gift from God, whereby he could interpret such engravings (p. 176, v. 28).
...Behold the virgin which thou seest, is the Mother of God (p. 25)	...Behold the virgin whom thou seest is the mother of the Son of God... (1 Nephi 11:18)
...that the Lamb of God is the eternal Father and the Saviour of the world... (p. 32)	...that the lamb of God is the Son of the Eternal Father...(1 Nephi 13:40).

The Book of Mormon and Archaeology

Mormon scholars can be frustrated and embarrassed understandably when they realize that after all the years of work by Mormon and other archaeologists:

1. No *Book of Mormon* cities have been located.
2. No *Book of Mormon* names have been found in New World inscriptions.
3. No genuine inscriptions have been found in Hebrew in America.
4. No genuine inscriptions have been found in America in Egyptian or anything similar to Egyptian, which could correspond to Joseph Smith's "reformed Egyptian."
5. No ancient copies of *Book of Mormon* scriptures have been found.
6. No ancient inscriptions of any kind in America which indicate that the ancient inhabitants had Hebrew or Christian beliefs have been found.
7. No mention of *Book of Mormon* persons, nations, or places have been found.
8. No artifact of any kind which demonstrates the *Book of Mormon* is true has been found.
9. Rather than finding supportive evidence, Mormon scholars have been forced to retreat from traditional interpretations of *Book of Mormon* statements (Hal Hougey, *Archaeology and the Book of Mormon*, p. 12).

Dr. Gleason Archer has done an excellent job in listing a few of the anachronisms and historical inaccuracies in the Mormon scriptures (*A Survey of Old Testament Introduction*, pp. 501-504):

In 1 Nephi 2:5-8, it is stated that the river Laman emptied into the Red Sea. Yet neither in historic nor prehistoric times has there been any river *in Arabia* at all that emptied into the Red Sea. Apart from an ancient canal which once connected the Nile with the coast of the Gulf of Suez, and certain wadis which showed occasional rainfall in ancient times, there were no streams of any kind emptying into the Red Sea on the western shore above the southern border of Egypt.

Second Nephi states that only the family of Lehi, Ishmael, and Zoram were left in Jerusalem in 600 B.C. to migrate to the New World. These totaled fifteen persons, plus three or four girls, or no more than twenty in all. Yet in less than thirty years, according to 2 Nephi 5:28, they had multiplied so startlingly that they divided up into two nations (2 Nephi 5:5-6, 21). Indeed, after arriving in America in 589 B.C., they are stated to have built a temple like Solomon's.

Now Solomon's temple required 153,000 workers and 30,000 overseers (1 Ki. 5:13, 15; 6:1, 38; 9:20,21; 2 Ch 2:2, 17,18) in seven and a half years. It is difficult to see how a few dozen unskilled workers (most of whom must have been children) could have duplicated this feat even in the nineteen years they allegedly did the work. Nor is it clear how all kinds of iron, copper, brass, silver, and gold could have been found in great abundance (2 Nephi 5:15) for the erection of this structure back in the sixth-century B.C. America.

According to Alma 7:10, Jesus was to be born at Jerusalem (rather than in Bethlehem, as recorded in Lk. 2:4 and predicted in Mic. 5:2).

Helamen 14:20, 27 states that darkness covered the whole earth for three *days* at the time of Christ's death (rather than three hours, as recorded in Mt. 27:45 and Mk. 15:33), or beyond Easter morning, which would have made it impossible for the woman at the tomb to tell whether the stone had been rolled away from its mouth.

Alma 46:15 indicates that believers were called "Christians" back in 73 B.C. rather than at Antioch, as Acts 11:26 informs us. It is difficult to imagine how anyone could have been labeled Christian so many decades before Christ was even born.

Helaman 12:25,26, allegedly written in 6 B.C., quotes John 5:29 as a prior written source, introducing it by the words, "We read." It is difficult to see how a quotation could be cited from a written source not composed until eight or nine decades after 6 B.C.

Quite numerous are the instances in which the Mormon scriptures, said to have been in the possession of the Nephites back in 600 B.C., quote from or allude to passages or episodes found only in exilic or postexilic books of the Old Testament. Several examples follow.

1. First Nephi 22:15 states: "For behold, saith the prophet, the time cometh speedily that Satan shall have no more power over the hearts of the children of men; for the day soon cometh that all the proud and they who do wickedly shall be as stubble; and the day cometh that they must be burned." Compare this with Malachi 4:1 (ca. 435 B.C.): "For, behold, the day cometh, that shall burn as an oven;

and all the proud, yea, and all that do wickedly, shall be stubble: and the day that cometh shall burn them up, saith the Lord of hosts, that it shall leave them neither root nor branch."

2. Second Nephi 26:9: "But the Son of righteousness shall appear unto them; and he shall heal them, and they shall have peace with him, until three generations shall have passed away." Compare this with Malachi 4:2: "But unto you that fear my name shall the Sun of righteousness arise with healing in his wings; and ye shall go forth and grow up as calves of the stall." Note the confusion between *Son* and *Sun*, which could only have originated from their similar sound in the English language.

3. Third Nephi 28:21-22: "And thrice they were cast into a furnace and received no harm. And twice they were cast into a den of wild beasts; and behold they did play with the beasts as a child with a suckling lamb, and received no harm." Compare this with Daniel 3 and 6 where such adventures befell Shadrach, Meshach and Abednego, along with Daniel himself. It is difficult to understand how these Mormon believers could have had experiences just like those related in the book of Daniel, which was not even composed until several decades after their alleged departure for the New World in 589 B.C. (Daniel could have found written form only after the fall of Babylon to the Persians in 539 B.C., since it contains at least fifteen Persian loanwords.)

4. Alma 10:2 states that Aminadi "interpreted the writing which was upon the wall of the temple, which was written by the finger of God." Surely this is a reminiscence of Daniel's feat in reading the divine handwriting upon the wall of Belshazzar's banquet hall in 539 B.C.

Even more remarkable is the abundance of parallels or word-for-word quotations from the *New* Testament which are found in the Book of Mormon, which was allegedly in the possession of the Nephites back in 600 B.C. Jerald and Sandra Tanner (*The Case Against Mormonism*, Vol. 2, Salt Lake City, 1967, pp. 87-102) have listed no less than 400 clear examples out of a much larger number that could be adduced; and these serve to establish beyond all question that the author of the Book of Mormon was actually well acquainted with the New Testament, and specifically in the KJV of 1611. A few examples follow:

1. 1 Nephi 4:13: "That one man could perish than that a nation should...perish in unbelief." Compare this with

John 11:50: "That one man should die for the people, and that the whole nation perish not."

2. 1 Nephi 10:8: "Whose shoe's latchet I am not worthy to unloose." Compare this with John 1:27: "Whose shoe's latchet I am not worthy to unloose."

3. 1 Nephi 10:9: "In Bethabara beyond Jordan...he should baptize." Compare this with John 1:28: "In Bethabara beyond Jordan, where John was baptizing."

4. 1 Nephi 11:22: "The love of God, which sheddeth itself abroad in the hearts of the children of men." Compare this with Romans 5:5: "The love of God is shed abroad in our hearts by the Holy Ghost."

5. 1 Nephi 11:27: "The Holy Ghost come down out of heaven and abide upon him in the form of a dove." Compare this with Luke 3:22: "The Holy Ghost descended in bodily shape like a dove upon him."

6. 1 Nephi 14:11: "The whore of all the earth, and she sat upon many waters; and she had dominion over all the earth, among all nations, kindreds, tongues, and people." Compare this with Revelation 17:1, 15: "The great whore sitteth upon many waters...The waters which thou sawest, where the whore sitteth, are peoples, and multitudes, and nations, and tongues."

Most interesting is the recently exposed fraud of the so-called Book of Abraham, part of the Mormon scripture known as *The Pearl of Great Price*. This was assertedly translated from an ancient Egyptian papyrus found in the mummy wrappings of certain mummies which had been acquired by a certain Michael H. Chandler.

In 1835 Joseph Smith became very much interested in these papyrus leaves, which he first saw in Kirtland, Ohio, on July 3, and arranged for the purchase of both mummies and manuscripts. Believing he had divinely received the gift of interpreting ancient Egyptian, he was delighted to find that one of the rolls contained the writings of Abraham himself, whose signature he had personally inscribed in the Egyptian language.

In 1842, Smith published his translation under the title, "The Book of Abraham" in *Times and Seasons*. He even included three drawings of the pictures or vignettes appearing in the manuscript, and interpreted the meaning of these illustrations: Abraham sitting upon the throne of Pharaoh, the serpent with walking legs who tempted Eve in Eden.

For many years this collection of papyri was lost, but somehow they (or else a duplicate set of them from ancient times) were presented to the Mormon Church by the

Metropolitan Art Museum of New York City on November 27, 1967. This made the translation skill of Joseph Smith susceptible of objective verification.

The unhappy result was that earlier negative verdicts of scholars like Theodule Devaria of the Louvre, and Samuel A. B. Mercer of Western Theological Seminary, and James H. Breasted of the University of Chicago, and W. F. Flinders Petrie of London University (who had all been shown Smith's facsimiles) were clearly upheld by a multitude of present-day Egyptologists.

Their finding was that not a single word of Joseph Smith's alleged translation bore any resemblance to the contents of this document. It turned out to be a late, even Ptolemaic, copy in hieratic script of the Sensen Papyrus, which belongs to the same genre as the Egyptian Book of the Dead.

As John A. Wilson, professor of Egyptology at the University of Chicago, described it in a published letter written on March 16, 1966, it contains vignettes familiar from the Book of the Dead. The first illustration shows the god of embalming named Anubis preparing the body of the deceased for burial, with the soul hovering over his head in the form of a bird, and the canopic jars containing the dead man's inwards set beneath his bier.

The third picture shows the deceased led into the presence of Osiris, the infernal deity who judged the souls of the dead. (This is what Smith had identified as Abraham sitting on Pharaoh's throne!). Figure 2 was a round disc made of cloth and jesso and customarily placed as a pillow under the head of a corpse in the Late Egyptian period.

The accompanying text, as can be ascertained from other copies of this not uncommon document, deals with magical spells intended to open the mouth of the deceased and to prepare him for his audience before Osiris in the judgment hall of the dead (as set forth in detail in chap. 125 of the Book of the Dead, the Egyptian title of which is *P-r m h-r-w*, or, "The Going Forth by Day"). Needless to say, the completely mistaken concept of Joseph Smith as to his competence in ancient Egyptian is now clearly demonstrated to be beyond debate.

False Prophecies

The Mormon religion contains false prophecies. 2 Nephi 10:7, speaking of the Jews, predicts, "...When the day cometh that they shall believe in me, that I am Christ, then have I covenanted with their fathers that they shall be restored in the flesh, upon the earth, unto the lands of their inheritance." The Jews are today back in their land, but do not believe that Jesus is the Christ. The prophecy is false.

Building the Temple in Zion

Joseph claimed that the Lord told him the Latter-Day Saints would build a temple in Zion (Jackson County, Missouri) during his generation. Zion would never be removed from its place. "...This generation shall not all pass away until an house shall be built unto the Lord...upon the consecrated spot as I have appointed" (*Doctrine and Covenants*, 84:5, 31, September 1832).

"Surely Zion is the city of our God, and surely Zion can not fall, neither be moved out of place, for God is there, and the hand of the Lord is there..." (*Doctrine and Covenants*, 97:19, August 1833).

These two prophecies failed since a temple was never built at the "appointed" place. Moreover, two weeks *before* Joseph gave the prophecy that Zion would not be "moved out of her place" the Mormons were unceremoniously run out of Zion. Their printing presses were destroyed, and some of their leaders were tarred and feathered! Joseph was in Kirtland, Ohio at that time and thus was ignorant of the situation in Jackson County, Missouri, when he uttered his prophecy. Later on that year Smith prophesied a return to Zion!

> Zion shall not be moved out of her place, notwithstanding her children are scattered. They that remain and are pure in heart, shall return and come to their inheritances, they and their children, with songs of everlasting joy, to build up the waste places of Zion—And all these things that the prophets might be fulfilled.
>
> And, behold, there is none other place appointed than that which I have appointed; neither shall there be any other placed appointed than that which I have appointed for the work of the gathering of my saints—Until the day cometh when there is found no more room for them; and then I have other places which I will appoint unto them, and they shall be called stakes, for the curtains or the strength of Zion (*Doctrine and Covenants* 101:17-21, 1833).

This is yet another false prophecy. It has been about 150 years since this "revelation" was given and a temple still has not been built on that site. Joseph said, "There is none other place appointed" and that it would be built during "his generation." He has failed all requirements of being a true prophet.

The God of the Bible never prophesies falsely. What He declares always comes to pass. Deuteronomy 13:1-4 and 18:18-22 gives us the two best tests of a self-proclaimed prophet. Deuteronomy 13 warns that a prophet, even if his prophecies come true, must lead you to believe in Jehovah God, the God of the Bible, or he is a false prophet. One who leads you to follow false gods is a false prophet and was to be stoned to death under the Old Testament theocracy.

Deuteronomy 18 warns that a prophet must be right about his prophecies every single time, or he is not a true prophet of God. The Mormon prophets fail the biblical tests of a prophet from God. Their prophecies are not from the Lord, and "the prophet has spoken presumptuously; you shall not be afraid of him" (v. 22).

Conclusion

When all the evidence is considered, the Mormon claim to be the restoration of Jesus Christ's church falls to the ground. We have taken up the challenge of Brigham Young who said, "Take up the Bible, compare the religion of the Latter-day Saints with it, and see if it will stand the test" (*Journal of Discourses*, Volume 16, p. 46, 1873).

Orson Pratt echoed the same sentiment, "Convince us of our errors of Doctrine, if we have any, by reason, by logical arguments, or by the Word of God and we will ever be grateful for the information and you will ever have the pleasing reflections that you have been instruments in the hands of God of redeeming your fellow beings" (*The Seer*, p. 15).

Our conclusion is that when Mormonism is weighed in the balances it is found wanting.

Mormonism Terms

Aaronic Priesthood—One of the two Mormon priesthoods into which Mormon leadership is divided. Includes the Presiding Bishopric, priests, teachers and deacons.

Adam — God — Said to be the God of this earth. Taught by second president, Brigham Young, now denied by LDS church.

Apostles — In Mormonism there are twelve apostles in the Melchizedek Priesthood, who are subordinate to everyone but the President of the Mormon Church.

Atonement — Jesus' atonement is not sufficient to cleanse all sins. Some sins must be atoned for by the individual. Early LDS teachings said one's own blood was to be spilt for such atonement.

Baptism for the Dead — Since LDS believes baptism is necessary for salvation, even the dead must be baptized by proxy, performed by living relatives.

Book of Abraham — Part of the Mormon sacred work *The Pearl of Great Price*, which contains the Mormon teachings that the black race is cursed.

Book of Mormon — One of the four sacred books of the Mormons containing a supposed history of the former inhabitants of America. It was supposedly translated from the golden plates.

Celestial Heaven — The highest of the three heavens in Mormon teaching.

Cumorah — The hill near Palmyra, New York where Joseph Smith, Jr. allegedly found the golden plates from which he translated the *Book of Mormon.*

Doctrine and Covenants — One of the four sacred books of the Mormons containing many revelations given allegedly by God to Joseph Smith, Jr.

High Priests — In Mormonism, the fourth level of the Melchizedek Priesthood. Consists of the Mormon stake presidents.

Lamanites — According to the *Book of Mormon*, the ancestors of the American Indian and their spiritual activities.

Living Prophets — In Mormonism, the current president of the Mormon church supposedly has the ability to receive divine revelations and is considered a "living prophet." His revelations are considered superior to all past revelations.

Lucifer — According to Mormonism, the spirit-brother of

Jesus. In Mormon theology Lucifer is the second-born creature of God after Jesus.

Manuscript Found — A novel (1812-1814) by Solomon Spaulding which many believe was later plagiarized by Joseph Smith to form the *Book of Mormon*.

Melchizedek Priesthood — The most important of the two Mormon priesthoods consisting of the presidency, apostles, patriarch, high priest, seventies, and elders.

Moroni — The angel who supposedly revealed the location of the golden plates to Joseph Smith, Jr. Smith translated them into the *Book of Mormon*.

Nephites — One of the groups of people who, according to the *Book of Mormon*, came to America from the Middle East.

Patriarch — The nominal head of Mormon hierarchy. It is an honorific title intially given to the father of the prophet.

Pearl of Great Price — One of the four sacred books of the Mormons containing, among other things, the *Book of Abraham* which teaches that the black race is cursed.

Presiding Bishopric — In Mormonism, the first division of the Aaronic Priesthood designated. The bishopric administers the local congregations, called wards.

Smith, Joseph Jr. (1805-1855) — Founder of the Church of Jesus Christ of Latter-day Saints (Mormon). Supposedly received a vision from God the Father informing him of certain golden plates which gave an account of the former inhabitants of America. Smith translated these plates which became the *Book of Mormon*.

Telestial Kingdom — Lowest division of glory (heaven) in Mormonism, reserved for those having no belief in Christ or the gospel.

Terrestrial Kingdom — a secondary degree of glory (heaven) reserved for those who, though honorable, failed to comply with the requirements of exaltation to Godhood.

Young, Brigham — Second president and successor to Joseph Smith, Jr., founder of the Church of Jesus Christ of Latter-day Saints (Mormon). Led the Mormons westward to Salt Lake City, Utah, where church is still headquartered.

CHAPTER SEVEN

Transcendental Meditation

History

The founder of TM, Mahesh Brasad Warma, later known as Maharishi Mahesh Yogi, was born in India around 1910. After graduating from Allahabad University in 1942 with a degree in physics, Mahesh became the disciple of the Indian religious leader Guru Dev. It was Guru Dev who taught Mahesh a meditation technique derived from the Vedas (part of the Hindu scripture).

The Maharishi (as he is referred to) was devoted to fulfilling the plan of Guru Dev in bringing his teachings to the world. In 1958 Maharishi founded the Spiritual Regeneration Movement in India. He came to America the following year and set up his organization while spreading the gospel of Guru Dev. Today, several million people in the United States and around the world have been taught the Maharishi's meditation techniques, said to be nonreligious, although thoroughly Hindu.

The Claims of TM

How would you like to have your health improved, your self-image and productivity increased, and your intelligence and creativity heightened without stress or tension?

According to its advertisements, these are some of the ways TM will benefit individuals. Allegedly all this can be done within any religious or nonreligious system since

TM supposedly has no religious basis. Moreover, TM has developed some very admirable goals to accomplish this in the lives of people by setting up nationwide centers.

Under a World Plan, 350 teaching centers of the Science of Creative Intelligence have been founded in the largest cities throughout the United States and the world. In fact, resolutions drawn up by the Maharishi and promoting TM have been adopted by legislatures throughout the country.

TM can appeal to all segments of society, including the famous (such as the Beatles in the mid-60's), the counter-culture, the business community and the intelligentsia. Stanford law professor John Kaplan testifies, "I use it the way I'd use a product of our technology to overcome nervous tension. It's a non-chemical tranquilizer with no unpleasant side effects" (*Time Magazine*, October 30, 1975).

TM, however, is not a neutral discipline that can be practiced without harm to the individual. In actuality, TM is a Hindu meditation technique that attempts to unite the meditator with Brahman, the Hindu concept of God.

The Religious Nature of TM

Despite claims to the contrary, TM is religious in nature. The following is a translation of the Puja, the initiation ceremony read in Sanskrit by the TM in-structor.

PUJA

Whether pure or impure, whether purity or impurity is permeating everywhere, whoever opens himself to the ex-panded vision of unbounded awareness gains inner and outer purity.

Invocation

To Lord Narayana, to lotus-born Brahma the Creator, to Vashishta, to Shakti, and to his son, Parashar, to Vyasa, to Shukadava, to the great Gaudapada, to Govinda, ruler among yogies, to his disciple, Shri Trotika and Varttika-Kara, to others, to the tradition of our masters I bow down. To the abode of the wisdom of the Shrutis, Smritis and Puranas, to the abode of kindness, to the personified glory of the Lord, to Shankara, emancipator of the Lord, I bow down. To Sharkaracharya, the redeemer, hailed as Krishna and

Badarayana, to the commentator of the Brahma Sutras, I bow down again and again. At whose door the whole galaxy of gods pray for perfection day and night, adorned with immeasurable glory, perceptor of the whole world, having bowed down to him, we gain fulfillment. Skilled in dispelling the cloud of ignorance of the people, the gentle emancipator, Bramananda Saraswati — the supreme teacher, full of brilliance, him I bring to my awareness.

Offering

Offering the invocation to the lotus feet of Shri Guru Dev, I bow down.

Offering a seat to the lotus feet of Shri Guru Dev, I bow down.

Offering an ablution to the lotus feet of Shri Guru Dev, I bow down.

Offering a cloth to the lotus feet of Shri Guru Dev, I bow down.

Offering sandalpaste to the lotus feet of Shri Guru Dev, I bow down.

Offering rice to the lotus feet of Shri Guru Dev, I bow down.

Offering a flower to the lotus feet of Shri Guru Dev, I bow down.

Offering incense to the lotus feet of Shri Guru Dev, I bow down.

Offering light to the lotus feet of Shri Guru Dev, I bow down.

Offering water to the lotus feet of Shri Guru Dev, I bow down.

Offering fruits to the lotus feet of Shri Guru Dev, I bow down.

Offering water to the lotus feet of Shri Guru Dev, I bow down.

Offering betel leaf to the lotus feet of Shri Guru Dev, I bow down.

Offering coconut to the lotus feet of Shri Guru Dev, I bow down.

Offering camphor light.

White as camphor, kindness incarnate, the essence of creation, garlanded with Brahman, ever dwelling in the lotus of my heart, the creative impulse of cosmic life, to that in the form of Guru Dev, I bow down.

Offering camphor light to the lotus feet of Shri Guru Dev, I bow down.

Offering water to the lotus feet of Shri Guru Dev, I bow down.

Offering a handful of flowers.

Guru in the glory of Brahma, guru in the glory of Vishnu, guru in the glory of the great Lord Shiva, guru in the glory of personified transcendental fullness of Brahman, to him Shri Guru Dev, adorned with glory, I bow down. The unbounded, like the endless canopy of the sky, by whom the moving and unmoving universe is pervaded, by whom the sign of That has been revealed, to him to Shri Guru Dev, I bow down. Guru Dev, Shri Brahmananda, bliss of the absolute, transcendental joy, the self-sufficient, the embodiment of pure knowledge which is beyond and above the universe like the sky, the goal of "thou art That" and other such expressions which unfold eternal truth, the one, the eternal, the pure, the immovable, to the very being of that which is the witness of all intellects, whose status transcends thought, the transcendent along with the three gunas, the teacher of the truth of the Absolute, to Shri Guru Dev, I bow down. To him by whom the blinding darkness of ignorance has been removed by applying the balm of knowledge; the eye of knowledge has been opened by him and therefore to him, to Shri Guru Dev, I bow down. Offering a handful of flowers to the lotus feet of Shri Guru Dev, I bow down. (*An English Translation of TM's Initiatory Puja*, Berkeley, Calif.: Spiritual Counterfeits Project, n.d.)

From the translation of the Puja, the religious nature of TM can clearly be seen. In 1977, a New Jersey federal court barred the teaching of TM in the schools of that state, the presiding judge concluding, "The teaching of SCI/TM and the Puja are religious in nature; no other inference is permissible or reasonable...although defendants have submitted well over 1500 pages of briefs, affidavits and deposition testimony in opposing plaintiffs' motion for summary judgment, defendants have failed to raise the slightest doubt as to the facts or as to the religious nature of the teaching of the Science of Creative Intelligence and the Puja. The teachings of SCI/TM courses in New Jersey violates the establishment clause of the First Amendment, and its teaching must be enjoined" (United States District Court, District of New Jersey, Civil Action No. 76-341). Therefore the claim of the Maharishi and his followers as to the non-religious basis of TM has no basis in fact.

Is It Harmless?

"The TM program has no adverse side effects and can promote what pills cannot — natural psychological growth" (Harold Bloomfield, meditator and psychiatrist, *TM: Overcoming Stress and Discovering Inner Energy*, p. 149).

There are, however, some authorities that would disagree with Bloomfield's statement.

> That the dangers of meditation are considerable among the immature appear to be overlooked by these (TM) enthusiasts who regard meditation as a universal panacea (Una Kroll, M.D., *London Times*, June 30, 1973).
>
> There are risks in cultivating altered states of consciousness. One of these risks...may be a permanent alienation from ordinary human attachments (Elsa First, child psychotherapist, *Frontiers of Consciousness*, p. 65, John White, ed.).
>
> As a person enters or is in an ASC (altered state of consciousness), he often experiences fear of losing his grip on reality, and losing his self-control (Arnold M. Ludwig, *Altered States of Consciousness*, p. 16, Charles Tart, ed.).

The Maharishi

Many of the statements made by the Maharishi concerning the Science of Creative Intelligence and the Age of Enlightenment are disturbing:

> There has not been and there will not be a place for the unfit. The fit will lead, and if the unfit are not coming along, there is no place for them. In the place where light dominates there is no place for darkness. In the age of Enlightenment there is no place for ignorant people. the ignorant will be made enlightened by a few orderly, enlightened people moving around. Nature will not allow ignorance to prevail. It just can't. Nonexistence of the unfit has been the law of nature (Maharishi, *Inauguration of the Dawn of the Age of Enlightenment*, MIU Press, p. 47).
>
> The Science of Creative Intelligence structures all knowledge in the awareness of everyone and thereby makes everyone infallible (ibid., p. 49).
>
> It is only childish and ridiculous to base one's life on the level of thinking. Thinking can never be a profound basis of living. Being is the natural basis...thinking, on the other

hand, is only imaginary (Maharishi, *Transcendental Meditation*, p.99).

It is disturbing to think that Maharishi would eliminate opposers and that thinking is useless! The Bible says that judgment belongs only to the Lord Jesus Christ (John 5:22, 27) and that one should examine and test all things by God's Word (1 John 4:1).

The Religious Beliefs of TM

We have already observed that TM is religious in nature, based upon Hinduism, consequently their theology is in direct contrast to Christianity.

God

The Maharishi's view of God reflects a denial of the infinite-personal God revealed in Scripture. He writes, "God is found in two phases of reality: as a supreme being of absolute, eternal nature and as a personal God at the highest level of phenomenal creation" (*Science of Being and Art of Living*, Maharishi Mahesh Yogi, Rev. Ed. 1967, p. 271).

This "supreme being" is identified with nature: "Everything in creation is the manifestation of the un-manifested absolute impersonal being, the omnipresent God" (Maharishi Mahesh Yogi, *Transcendental Meditation*, p. 266). "This impersonal God is that being which dwells in the heart of everyone" (ibid, p. 269).

Man is also identified with God: "Each individual is, in his true nature, the impersonal God" (Maharishi Mahesh Yogi, *Science of Being and Art of Living*, Rev. Ed. 1967, p. 276). This same God is controlling evolution: "God, the supreme almighty being, in whose person the process of evolution finds its fulfillment, is on the top level of creation" (Maharishi Mahesh Yogi, *Transcendental Meditation*, p. 270). "He (God) maintains the entire field of evolution and the different lives of innumerable beings in the whole cosmos" (ibid, p. 271).

Maharishi's view of God and man is not in accord with the Bible. Scripture teaches that God is infinite while man is finite. Man can never become God or attain Godhood for he is part of God's creation. Man is the creature. God is the creator. Although man is part of God's creation, he is not to be identified with God. God, the creator, is a being separate from His creation. God is by nature eternal, whereas God's creation is temporal (it came into being at a particular time). Man, the finite, will never become God, the infinite.

Jesus Christ

The Maharishi does not have much to say about Jesus but when he does, he contradicts the Bible.

> Due to not understanding the life of Christ and not understanding the message of Christ, I don't think Christ ever suffered or Christ could suffer...It's a pity that Christ is talked of in terms of suffering...Those who count upon the suffering, it is a wrong interpretation of the life of Christ and the message of Christ...How could suffering be associated with the One who has been all joy, all bliss, who claims all that? It's only the misunderstanding of the life of Christ (Maharishi Mahesh Yogi, *Meditations of Maharishi Mahesh Yogi*, pp. 123-124).

It is the Maharishi who misunderstands the purpose of Christ's coming, which was to die for the sins of the world. "The next day he saw Jesus coming to him, and said, Behold, the Lamb of God who takes away the sin of the world!" (John 1:29 NASB), and "Just as the Son of man did not come to be served, but to serve, and to give His life a ransom for many" (Matthew 20:28 NASB). Jesus Christ, contrary to the teaching of the Maharishi, suffered on the cross for our sins so we might receive forgiveness from God for our sins. His suffering was real.

Conclusion

Transcendental Meditation (The Science of Creative Intelligence), though claiming to be a method of relaxation and personal growth without harmful side effects, can be a danger to the individual both emotionally and spiritually. Although some degree of success in relaxation can be achieved by practicing TM, the dangers far outweigh the benefits. There is a Christian alternative to TM and that consists of meditation on God's Word, the only source of real peace. No one said it better than the psalmist:

Blessed is the man that walketh not in the counsel of the ungodly, nor standeth in the way of sinners, nor sitteth in the seat of the scornful. But his delight is in the law of the LORD; and in his law doth he meditate day and night. And he shall be like a tree planted by the rivers of water, that bringeth forth his fruit in his season; his leaf also shall not wither; and whatsoever he doeth shall prosper. The ungodly are not so: but are like chaff which the wind driveth away. Therefore the ungodly shall not stand in the judgment, nor sinners in the congregation of the righteous. For the LORD knoweth the way of the righteous: but the way of the ungodly shall perish (Psalm 1:1-6).

Transcendental Meditation Terms

Transcendental Meditation—Hindu religious sect founded by Maharishi Mahesh Yogi under the guise of the supposedly nonreligious Science of Creative Intelligence. Promises to expand one's awareness and creativity.

American Foundation for the Science of Creative Intelligence—Pseudonym for TM organization.

Brahmins—The Hindu priestly class.

Guru Dev—The late Hindu Swami (religious master) who was the teacher of Maharishi Mahesh Yogi, the founder of TM. Dev is addressed as deity in the TM initiation ceremony.

International Meditation Society—Pseudonym for TM organization.

Maharishi Mahesh Yogi—The founder of Transcendental Meditation (TM).

Mantra—In Hinduism, a sacred word which embodies through some specific supernatural and spiritual power. Also used as the meditative words in TM.

Prana—In TM, it is the internal force within God by which He creates.

Puja—In TM, a written portion of the initiation ceremony read in Sanskrit by the instructor. It is a collection of prayers to Hindu deities.

Sanatana dharma—A Hindu term, referring to Hinduism as the eternal system, the one true religion.

Students International Meditation Society — Pseudonym for TM organization.

TM — Abbreviation for Transcendental Meditation.

Vedas — The collection of Hindu sacred scriptures.

Yoga — According to Hinduism, an exercise (physical, mental, or spiritual) designed to aid in one's progress to God-realization.

CHAPTER EIGHT

Theosophy

History

Theosophy literally means "wisdom of God." The modern Theosophical movement was founded in 1875 by Helena P. Blavatsky. The wisdom of God, according to Theosophists, is to be found in all religions: "What we desire to prove is, that underlying every once popular religion was the same ancient wisdom-doctrine, one and identical, professed and practiced by the initiates of every country who alone were aware of its existence and importance. To ascertain its origin and the precise way in which it was matured is now beyond human possibility" (A. P. Sinnett, *The Purpose of Theosophy*, Boston, 1888, p. 25).

Since there is truth in all religions, a Theosophist may pursue any religion he desires. This, however, did not stop Mrs. Blavatsky from detesting organized Christianity: "The name has been used in a manner so intolerant and dogmatic, especially in our day, that Christianity is now the religion of arrogance, par excellence, a stepping-stone for ambition, a sinecure for wealth, sham, and power; a convenient screen for hypocrisy" (H. P. Blavatsky, *Studies in Occultism*, Theosophical University Press, n.d., p. 138).

Source of Authority

There are no sacred books in Theosophy. Revelation

comes from "adepts," who are "beings perfected spiritually, intellectually, and physically, the flower of human and all evolution" (*The Theosophical Movement*, p. 112). Mrs. Blavatsky was the first individual in Theosophy who received messages from these adepts and passed them on to the world.

The Teachings of Theosophy

A few sample quotations from Theosophical writings demonstrate their non-Christian character.

God

"We reject the idea of a personal...God" (H. P. Blavatsky, *Key to Theosophy*, Point Loma, California, Aryan Theosophical Press, 1913).

"We believe in a universal divine principle, the root of all, from which all proceeds, and within which all shall be absorbed at the end of the great cycle of being" (ibid., p. 63).

The rejection of a personal God is a rejection of the God of the Bible, the infinite-personal creator. Theosophy has no room for a God who has created man in His personal image: "Then God said, let us make man in Our image to Our likeness..." (Genesis 1:26 NASB).

Man

Theosophists teach that man consists of seven parts: 1. The body; 2. Vitality; 3. Astral body; 4. Animal soul; 5. Human soul; 6. Spiritual soul; and 7. Spirit. "Man is also equated with God, "...for you are God, and you will only what God wills; but you must dig deep down into yourself to find the God within you and listen to His voice which is your voice" (Krishnamurti, *At the Feet of the Master*, p. 10).

Man is evolving individually and corporately. Salvation is achieved when man's seventh stage is attained involving progressing from one body to another based upon his own self-effort. This is similar to the eastern doctrine of the law of Karma.

There is nothing in Scripture to suggest that man has a seven-part constitution. Rather he consists of body, soul and spirit, "Now may the God of peace Himself sanctify you entirely; and may your spirit and soul and body be preserved complete, without blame at the coming of our Lord Jesus Christ" (1 Thessalonians 5:23 NASB).

Jesus Christ

"...for Christ — — — the true esoteric saviour — — — is no man but the DIVINE PRINCIPLE in every human being" (H. P. Blavatsky, *Studies in Occultism*, Theosophical University Press, n.d., p. 134).

Mrs. Blavatsky, sounding like Christian Science, attempts to separate Christ from the person Jesus. However, Christ is merely his title, meaning "anointed one" or "messiah," designating the office Jesus held. There is no justification for making any distinction between Jesus and "The Christ." Furthermore, making Christ a principle rather than a true man is a denial of the whole purpose of His coming: "And the word became flesh and dwelt amongst us" (John 1:14 KJV).

Reincarnation

"No one is to blame except ourselves for our birth conditions, our character, our opportunities, our abilities, for all these things are due to the working out of forces we have set going either in this life or in former lives..." (Irving S. Cooper, *Theosophy Simplified*, p. 55).

The idea of reincarnation, that people must go through a series of lives to atone for their sins, is a denial of the work of Christ accomplished on the cross. Salvation has been made complete by Christ's sacrifice. There is nothing any of us can do to add or subtract from it. Consequently, there is no need for a series of births to accomplish what Christ has already completed.

The Afterlife

There is no heaven or hell as such in Theosophy. The Theosophist can reach a state of "nirvana" in which the individual is absorbed by the impersonal world, losing all personal consciousness.

The Bible teaches that there is an existence after death for everyone. Those who have put their trust in Jesus

Christ will forever reside in God's presence while those who reject Christ will spend eternity apart from him. John's gospel makes this plain: "He who believes in the Son has eternal life; but he who does not obey the Son shall not see Life, but the wrath of God abides on him" (John 3:36 NASB).

The Bible

"I confined myself to the Hindu Scriptures, and in all cases I stated that I regarded these scriptures and the Hindu religion as the origin of all scriptures and all religions" (Annie Besant, *The Daily Chronicle*, April 9, 1894).

This statement totally denies the basic premise of the Christian faith, namely, that God has given the world a unique revelation concerning who He is and who we are (Hebrews 1:1-3). The Bible cannot be God's inspired word if its origin is found in Hinduism.

Conclusion

When Theosophy beliefs are examined, we discover the whole Theosophical system is contrary to Christianity. There is, therefore, no possibility of reconciliation between the two, since the followers of Theosophy extol Buddhist and Brahmanic theories, and Christians follow Jesus Christ alone.

Theosophy Terms

Theosophy—Literally means "wisdom of God." Theosophy is a cult founded by Helena Blavatsky in 1875 and which attempts to expound on the wisdom of God found in all religions. Occultic practices are used within the group.

Adept—In Theosophy, a being from the spirit world who communicates revelations. Also known as Bodhisattva or Mahatma.

Animal Soul—The fourth principle of human nature, according to Theosophy. The majority of people alive today are at this level.

Atlantean—According to Theosophy, it is the second of three levels thus far reached in human evolution.

Besant, Annie — British woman who was a highly influential leader in Theosophy as a successor to founder Helena Blavatsky. In 1906 she publicly announced to the world the coming of the Messiah, Krishnamurti, whom she reared as a child. Krishnamurti later renounced his role.

Blavatsky, Helena Petrovna — (1831-1891). Founder of Theosophy. Incorporated occultic and eastern beliefs and practices together.

Devachan — The Theosophist's heaven.

Devas — Persons who, according to Theosophy, have been freed from their bodily prisons and are now in the world of the mind.

H.P.B. — Common designation in Theosophy for founder Helena P. Blavatsky.

Koot Hoomi — In Theosophy, one of the adepts who gave revelations to founder Madame Blavatsky.

Krishnamurti — Supposed Messiah figure in Theosophy who later renounced his role.

Leadbeater, C. W. — Along with Annie Besant, succeeded Helena Blavatsky in directing the Theosophical movement.

Mahatma — In Theosophy, an adept, a being from the spirit world who communicates through spiritually receptive living persons.

CHAPTER NINE

EST

History

"**B**ut don't get me wrong, I don't think the world needs EST; I don't think the world needs anything; the world already is and that's perfect."

"If nobody needs it then why do you do it?"

"I do it because I do it because that's what I do."

(Adam Smith, *"Powers of Mind, Part II: The EST Experience,"* New York, September 29, 1975, p. 284).

This statement is from an interview with former used car salesman John Paul Rosenberg, now known as Werner Erhard, founder and director of EST (Erhard Seminars Training) one of the fastest-growing movements in America. Thousands of people, including prominent public figures, have given glowing testimonies of the transforming effects of EST.

Dr. Herbert Hansher, psychology professor at Temple University, has called EST "one of the most powerful therapeutic experiences yet devised" (Adelaid Bry, *EST: 60 Hours that Transform Your Life*, New York: Avon, 1976, p. 200). Singer/Songwriter John Denver has said of his EST encounters, "It's the single most important experience of my life" (*Newsweek*, December 20, 1976).

Although not primarily religious in nature, EST denies the basic beliefs of the historic Christian faith, yet claims compatibility with Jesus Christ and Christianity. It is for this reason we treat EST with the non-Christian cults.

By way of background, Erhard (or Rosenberg) traveled the religious merry-go-round of Scientology, Zen Buddhism, yoga, hypnosis, Silva Mind Control and a host of other religious movements before presenting the world with EST in 1971 ("Werner Erhard — An Interview with the Source of EST" Part 1, *The New Age Journal*, No. 7, Sept. 15, 1975, pp. 18-20).

What is EST?

EST consists of 60 hours of intensive training, usually on two successive weekends, where the initiate attempts to reach the goal of EST: "getting it." It is, however, never clear exactly what one gets, for Erhard's system is a unique combination of Zen Buddhism, Scientology, and Vendanta Hinduism, coupled with the power of positive thinking.

Erhard has said, "We want nothing short of a total transformation — an alteration of substance, not a change of form" (Werner Erhard, *What's So*, Jan. 1975). This alteration or transformation is accomplished during the training sessions by attempting to change the individual's concept of who he is. Once a person's belief system is shredded, the person becomes vulnerable to accepting the ESTian world view.

The Philosophy of EST

Erhard's world view of life is perfect, with no difference between right and wrong. "Life is always perfect just the way it is. When you realize that, then no matter how strongly it may appear to be otherwise, you know that whatever is happening right now will turn out all right. Knowing this, you are in a position to begin mastering life" (Werner Erhard, *What's So*, January 1975). "Wrong is actually a version of right. If you are always wrong you are right" (Adelaide Bry, op. cit., p. 192).

Accordingly, there is no objective truth, no absolutes except the absolute of "whatever is, is right." With this viewpoint one could argue that anyone has the right to do whatever he wishes, including killing six million Jews, because he is perfect. Such a world view opens the door to frightening possibilities.

At the heart of the ESTian world view is the assumption that God is man and man is God, and that each individual must come to understand he is his own God. John Denver illustrated this assumption in his statement, "I can do anything. One of these days, I'll be so complete I won't be human, I'll be a god" (*Newsweek*, Dec. 20, 1976).

Erhard's seminars attempt to enlighten the uninitiated to this truth. As one EST trainer told his trainees, "It ought to be perfectly clear to everyone that you are all (expletive deleted) and I'm God. Only an (expletive deleted) would argue with God" (Luke Rhinehart, *The Book of EST*, New York: Holt Rhinehart and Winston, 1976, p. 47).

Seeing that all of us are God, we are now provided with justification to do whatever we please, since as God we are answerable to no one.

God

If indeed we ourselves are God, the need to look to a supreme being for salvation is gone, and the God of the Bible is unnecessary. Erhard has stated, "For instance, I believe that the belief in God is the greatest barrier to God in this universe — the single greatest barrier. I would prefer someone who is ignorant to someone who believes in God because the belief in God is a total barrier, almost a total barrier to the experience of God" (Werner Erhard, *East-West Journal*, September 1974).

The Bible reveals not only that man is not God, but that he can never become God. God is by nature infinite (unlimited) whereas man is finite (limited). God is the creator and man is the creature. We are dependent on Him for our very existence.

> The God who made the world and all things in it, since He is Lord of Heaven and earth, does not dwell in temples made with hands; neither is He served by human hands, as though he needed anything since He Himself gives to all life and breath and all things (Acts 17:24, 25 NASB).

Jesus Christ

Jesus supposedly was saying the same sort of thing as Erhard. Consequently in EST there is no need to give Jesus Christ any special adoration.

...the church totally misinterpreted what Jesus said. He kept telling over and over that everybody was like He was: perfect. He was experiencing life, like Werner. He knew He was the total source, living moment to moment, and was spontaneous.

Jesus is just another guru who happens to be popular here in Western Civilization. I can't go into a church and praise Jesus. But I really got where he is coming from. He wants to let everybody know "I'm you." So my whole point of view about religion has totally altered (Adelaid Bry, op. cit., p. 182).

It is difficult to understand how anyone who reads the Bible could believe Jesus said everyone was perfect. The truth is that Jesus said: "...for unless you believe that I am He, you shall die in your sins" (John 8:24 NASB). "For from within, out of the heart of men, proceed the evil thoughts, fornications, thefts, murders, adulteries, deeds of coveting and wickedness, as well as deceit, sensuality, envy, slander, pride and foolishness. All these evil things proceed from within and defile the man" (Mark 7:21-23).

Furthermore, as uniquely God in human flesh, Jesus deserves our worship, "...at the name of Jesus, every knee should bow, of those who are in heaven, and on earth, and under the earth, and that every tongue should confess that Jesus Christ is Lord to the glory of God the Father" (Philippians 2:10, 11).

Conclusion

The entire EST system centers around the self-centered individual rather than the biblical God. In EST, God is non-existent. Any religious or psychologically-manipulating system that leads people away from the true and living God is functioning as antichrist and should be avoided.

The experience EST offers is a pseudo-answer to man's deepest need. Only a personal relationship with Jesus Christ can truly satisfy the longing of the human heart. Jesus said, "If therefore the Son shall make you free you shall be free indeed" (John 8:36 NASB).

EST Terms

EST—Designation for Erhard Seminars Training,

advertised as a non-religious self-help training session designed to bring participants to fulfillment. Teaches that you are your own God, and that everything you experience (even bad things like assault) is a product of your own divine creative will.

Danger Process— One segment of EST's seminar.

Erhard, Werner— Founder of Erhard Seminars Training (EST). Born John Paul Rosenberg, Erhard experimented with a variety of groups including Silva Mind Control, Zen, and Scientology before forming his own self-help cult, EST.

Games— EST's name for the external world and its events. EST declares that the world of games is illusory. The only reality exists in the individual's mind.

Trainers— EST staff persons who conduct and teach the EST seminars.

Truth Process— One segment of EST's seminar.

Children of God

History

The founder of the original Children of God, now known as the Family of Love, is David Brandt Berg, born in Oakland, California, February 18, 1919. David Berg's parents were Virginia Brandt Berg, a prominent evangelist, and Mr. Berg, a minister with the Christian and Missionary Alliance. Eventually Mr. Berg's ministry was overshadowed by his wife's ministry, and he became part of her evangelistic team.

David Berg became a pastor with the Christian and Missionary Alliance Church sometime in the late 1940's. His first pastorate was in Arizona in 1949. However, a year later, in 1950, he left after a falling-out with the leadership of the church. This experience left him with great bitterness and permanent contempt for organized religion. His belief that God had a special destiny and mission for him developed shortly after this. In one publication, Berg recounted one of his early revelations:

> One of the first prophecies we ever received regarding my personal ministry was "I have made thee a sharp-toothed threshing instrument which shall beat the mountains as chaff and rip with violence the pillows from under the arms of them which sit at ease in Zion!" (Moses David, *The Disciple Revolution*, London: The Children of God, 1975, pp. 7, 8).

In 1968, with his wife Jane and their four children, Berg

moved to Huntington Beach, California. It was here that Berg developed a small following of people, basically from the counter-culture. In 1969, Berg became convinced that a great earthquake was imminent and California would slide into the Pacific Ocean. He and about 50 followers left California for Arizona where their disruption of church services and condemnation of organized churches resulted in their being asked to leave.

The group, now numbering 75, wandered across the United States and Canada, staging demonstrations along the way. It was during this time they adopted the name, "Children of God, and Berg took the name of Moses David, or "Mo." All converts take Bible names as a symbol of their "new birth."

In 1970, the group was allowed to use the facilities in Texas and California owned by T.V. evangelist Fred Jordan. Within the next one and a half years the group grew to 250. However, a disagreement arose between Jordan and the group at one of his properties and they were banished from all his properties. The Children of God then divided into small groups of fewer than 12 people and scattered across the country.

The Children of God, who now call themselves the Family of Love, boast about 7,000 members (including children) in approximately 80 countries. Since 1972, Berg has permanently resided in Europe where he oversees his group and writes his letters.

Source of Authority

There is no question as to who is the authority in the Children of God. It is David Berg, a man who considers himself to be a prophet for this generation. Members of the Children of God can receive God's truth only through "Father" Moses David:

> The structure (of the Children of God organization)...like a tree, with Jesus as its Root and Foundation Stump, your Prophet and King (David Berg as its chief administrator, with the sap of God's Word as its life's blood). (Moses David, *The New Leadership Revolution*, London: The Children of God, 1975, p. 2).

He communicates to his disciples by means of MO

letters, which are considered authoritative: "Do you want to know what the real avant-garde of this movement is? It's the MO letters! That's what is leading us all! All the general on the battlefield does is carry out the orders that come from higher up, from the Lord through MO!" (Faith David, *Pioneering, Popularity, and Persecution*, London: Children of God Trust, Oct. 25, 1973, DO #20, p. 5).

His "MO" letters are to be taken at face value:

We have heard of quite a few instances where leaders have changed the meaning of my letters by their actions or verbal interpretations. My letters mean exactly what they say, literally, and they don't need explaining away, spiritualizing or reinterpreting by anyone (Moses David, *Reorganization, Nationalization, Revolution!*, Rome: Children of God, Jan., 1978, DO #650).

The Beliefs of the Children of God

There has never been a statement of belief issued by the Children of God, so their views on theology must be gleaned from the vague and contradictory writings of Berg. Since it is difficult to systematize their beliefs about God, we will cite some of Berg's statements to give you a sample of their erratic nature:

"Well, if they believe in the virgin birth then they have got to believe in the divinity of Jesus, that He was partly God, even though according to some of their advocates they claim they don't. See they're contradicting their own Bible, because if He was virgin-born then He was the Son of God!

"Even so God createth what He willeth"—In other words He, Jesus, was a creation of God. Oh, this is exactly according to the Scriptures! Can you think of a verse on it? What does God's Word say about Jesus? It says that He was "the beginning of the creation of God!" (Rev. 3:14).

Now you know the Catholics and some are so strong on the so-called Trinity, but I don't even believe in the Trinity. You can't find that word in the Bible, so why should I believe it? But I believe in the Father and I believe in the Son, Jesus, and I believe in the Holy Ghost.

If you want to call it Trinity, all right, but I don't believe in it in some ways, the way some overemphasize and stress it, you know. You would think that Jesus just always was, just like God, but in a sense He was not until He was made man, although He was in the beginning and He was a part of God.

But God's Word also says that He was the beginning of the creation of God—you know where that's found? I recall it's in Revelation in the first two or three chapters there" (Moses David, *Islam*, [Ch. 1], Rome Children of God, May 18, 1975, Dfo, No. 631, p. 14).

Revolution

The Children of God is a revolutionary organization, emphasizing "forsaking all" for Jesus. This includes giving up of all material possessions to the group and the forsaking of their allegiance to families. Originally, Berg's message was one of dropping out of the corrupt system and joining God's system, the Children of God. Recently, however, he has emphasized that his followers should use the system for their own end, rather than totally dropping out. The following is a sample of what Berg has said about "the system":

> You, my dear parents, are the greatest rebels against God and his ways—not us, and unto you will be the greater condemnation; for how can we rebel against a God whom we know not, whose ways you never showed us, and you denied Him. You heard His Word, but heeded it not. You were shown His Ways, but followed them not...
>
> To hell with your devilish system. May God damn your unbelieving hearts. It were better that a millstone be hung around your neck and you be cast into the midst of the sea than to have caused one of these little ones to stumble. You were the real rebels, my dear parents, and the worst of all time. God is going to destroy you and save us, as we rebel against your wickedness, deny your ungodliness, break your unscriptural traditions and destroy your idolatrous System in the name of God almighty (Moses David, *The Revolutionary Rules*, London, Children of God, March 1972, GP No. S-RV, p. 1).

Sex

The writings of Berg are filled with references and allusions to unbiblical sex. Over the years his preoccupation with sex has become more and more noticeable in his writings. The sexual practices of the Children of God were exposed in an interview in *Christianity Today*, February 18, 1977, when Joseph Hopkins questioned two former members and leaders of the Children of God, Jack Wasson and David Jacks:

Hopkins: What about sex in the COG? There have been rumors of immorality and hanky-panky in the higher echelons. Are they true?

Jacks: Extramarital relationships, definitely. Berg cites Abraham, Solomon, David, and so on, as examples for his having concubines. The top leaders have sexual affairs with girls in the group. But the disciples are practically eunuchs for a year or so until they get married in the COG.

Wasson: This fooling around with sex goes way back. Married couples were encouraged as a group to participate in "skinny-dipping" — swimming in the nude. It was considered unrevolutionary not to participate. And COG members will do almost anything to avoid being called unrevolutionary. It was also policy for all married couples to attend evening "leadership training" sessions at the TSC (Texas Soul Clinic) Ranch in west Texas in the early days of the COG. These sessions would be led by David Berg, and no matter what subject they started out about, they always ended up on the subject of sex, with David Berg frequently leading the couples into a mass love-making session while he looked on. Then this doctrine came up that was taught only among the top leadership: "all things common," based on Acts 2:44. They applied the "all things" even to wives and husbands. The wife-and-husband-swapping was not explicitly condoned in a MO letter, but it was allowed and participated in by the top leadership.

Conclusion

Over the years the Children of God have strayed further and further away from the truth of the Gospel. Many misguided individuals, including some Christians, have joined this cult only to be misled by their false and un-biblical teachings. David Berg is not who he claims to be, God's prophet for this generation. Rather, he is a false prophet — "the blind leading the blind." Anyone who truly desires to serve God should not join this cult. They are indeed *not* the Children of God.

Children of God (Family of Love) Terms

Children of God (Family of Love) — Small cult founded by David "Moses" Berg in Southern California in 1968. Emphasizes forsaking all, including family, to follow Jesus.

Berg, David Brandt — Former fulltime worker with the Christian and Missionary Alliance Church. Berg was asked to leave his church and soon thereafter founded the Children of God in Huntington Beach, California. He took the designation Moses and considers himself a modern-day prophet.

COG — Designation for the Children of God cult.

Family of Love — Current name of the Children of God cult.

Father David — Pseudonym for David Berg, founder of the Children of God cult.

Flirty Fishing (Ffing) — Term used by the Children of God cult referring to the use of sex to entice people to join or contribute to their cult.

King David — Pseudonym for David Berg, founder of the Children of God cult.

Litnessing — Term used by the Children of God referring to the passing out of literature in exchange for donations.

MO Letters — Letters written by David "Moses" Berg, leader of the Children of God, to his followers. These letters are considered by the Children of God members as scripture on the same level of inspiration as both the Old and New Testaments.

Moses David — Pseudonym for David Berg, founder of the Children of God cult.

The New Nation News — Periodical published by the Children of God cult.

CHAPTER ELEVEN

The Unification Church "Moonies"

The founder and leader of the Unification Church is Sun Myung Moon who was born in Korea on January 6, 1920. His family converted to Christianity when he was ten and became members of the Presbyterian Church.

The Vision

At age 16 young Moon experienced a vision while in prayer on a Korean mountainside. Moon claims that Jesus Christ appeared to him in the vision admonishing him to carry out the task that Christ had failed to complete. Jesus supposedly told Moon that he was the only one who could do it. Finally, after much repeated asking by Jesus, Moon accepted the challenge.

Moon spent the next few years of his life preparing for the great spiritual battle ahead. The years between his "conversion" experience and his coming to America are shrouded in much controversy. For documentation on those intervening years we would recommend *The Moon is Not the Son* by James Bjornstad, Minneapolis: Dimension Books/Bethany House Press, 1976.

Moon Comes to America

After achieving success with his new religion in the Far East, especially South Korea, Moon came to America at the end of 1971 and his cult began to flourish. Today they claim some two million members worldwide.

The Claims of Sun Myung Moon

Sun Myung Moon has made it clear that he believes himself to be the Messiah for this age.

> With the fulness of time, God has sent his messenger to resolve the fundamental questions of life and the universe. His name is Sun Myung Moon. For many decades, he wandered in a vast spiritual world in search of ultimate truth. On this path he endured suffering unimagined by anyone in human history...He fought alone against myriads of satanic forces in both the spiritual and physical worlds, and finally triumphed over them all. In this way, he came in contact with many saints in paradise and with Jesus, and thus brought into Light all the heavenly secrets through his communion with God (Sun Myung Moon, *Divine Principle*, p. 16).

Moon has also said, "No heroes in the past, no saints or holy men in the past, like Jesus or Confucius, have excelled us" (Sun Myung Moon, "Our Shame," translated by Won Pok Choi, from *Master Speaks*, March 11, 1973, p. 3).

Even though Moon's doctrines are opposed to Christianity, he claims that it was Jesus who revealed them to him. "You may again want to ask me, 'With what authority do you weigh these things?' I spoke with Jesus Christ in the spirit world. And I spoke also with John the Baptist. This is my authority. If you cannot at this time determine that my words are the truth, you will surely discover that they are in the course of time. These are hidden truths presented to you as a new revelation. You have heard me speak the Bible. If you believe the Bible, you must believe what I am saying" (Rev. Moon, *Christianity in Crisis*, p. 98).

And, like all cult leaders, Moon claims exclusive knowledge. "We are the only people who truly understand the heart of Jesus, and the hope of Jesus" (Rev. Moon, *The Way of the World*, p. 20).

Source of Authority

In the Unification Church the writings and teachings of

Moon take precedence over the Bible, "It may be displeasing to religious believers, especially to Christians, to learn that a new expression of truth must appear. They believe that the Bible, which they now have, is perfect and absolute in itself" (*Divine Principle*, 2nd ed., 1973, p. 9).

Moon further stated, "...The New Testament Words of Jesus and the Holy Spirit will lose their light...to 'lose their light' means that the period of their mission has elapsed with the coming of the new age" (*Divine Principle*, p. 118). The basic work containing the supposed revelations given to Moon is entitled the *Divine Principle*.

The Divine Principle

For the members of the Unification Church, the *Divine Principle* is the ultimate authoritative work, superseding even the Bible. The *Divine Principle* is known as the completed testament because it supposedly contains the present truth for this age which heretofore had never been revealed.

The assertions of Moon are at complete odds with the Bible. The Scriptures testify that the Word of God is eternal: "The grass withers, the flower fades, but the Word of God stands forever" (Isaiah 40:8 NASB). Jesus said, "Heaven and earth shall pass away, but my Words shall not pass away " (Matthew 24:35). The idea that the words of Jesus will somehow lose their light is totally foreign to the teaching of the Bible.

Moreover, the Bible records the strongest condemnation for those who would add to what the Scriptures have revealed, "You shall not add to the Word which I am commanding you, nor take away from it. That you may keep the commandments of the Lord your God which I command you" (Deuteronomy 4:2 NASB). "I testify to everyone who hears the words of the prophecy of this book; if anyone adds to them, God shall add to him the plagues which are written in this book" (Revelation 22:18 NASB).

Furthermore, the Scriptures make it plain that the faith has been "once for all delivered to the saints" (Jude 3). Any so-called revelation that contradicts that which was previously revealed is guilty of adding to the Word of God and should be discarded. The *Divine Principle* is in this category.

Unification Doctrine

Basic to Moon's world view is the concept of dualism. All of existence is dual: Father God and Mother God; Male and Female; Light and Dark; Yin and Yang; Spirit and Flesh. Each part of existence has its dual aspect. Moon's God (with dual male/female aspects) always acts in a dual manner with his dual creation.

The Fall of Man

According to the *Divine Principle*, until now no one has correctly understood the Genesis account of the fall of man. The *Divine Principle* teaches there were two falls, one physical and one spiritual. Moreover, both falls were sexual in nature. Eve supposedly had an illicit sexual relationship with Lucifer causing the spiritual fall. Afterward, her sexual relationship with spiritually immature Adam resulted in the physical fall.

The *Divine Principle* justifies this by saying, "It is the nature of man to conceal an area of transgression. They covered their sexual parts, clearly indicating that they were ashamed of the sexual areas of their bodies because they had committed sin through them" (*Divine Principle*, p. 72).

Since there was a dual aspect of the fall there also needs to be a dual aspect of redemption, necessitating both physical and spiritual salvation.

The Coming of Christ

When Jesus Christ came to earth, He was supposed to redeem mankind both physically and spiritually, but He failed in His mission: "Jesus failed in His Christly mission. His death on the cross was not an essential part of God's plan for redeeming sinful man" (*Divine Principle*, pp. 142, 143).

The ministry of Christ, however, was not a total failure for He did accomplish a "spiritual" salvation at the cross of Calvary, but He failed in achieving a "physical salvation" for mankind (*Divine Principle*, p. 151).

John the Baptist

Moon believes the major reason for Jesus' crucifixion was John the Baptist's failure. John was supposed to clear the way for Jesus to come to the people of his day but failed because he lost faith. This caused the people to abandon Jesus and eventually resulted in His death. The crucifixion was not something God desired because the work of Christ was unfinished. It is here where Sun Myung Moon picks up where Jesus left off. Moon is supposedly the "third Adam," the one who is called to redeem mankind physically.

Jesus Christ

Moon has a non-biblical view of the person of Jesus Christ by denying the unique deity of Jesus Christ.

"Jesus is the man of this value. However great his value may be, he cannot assume any value greater than that of a man..." (Rev. Moon, *Divine Principle*, p. 255).

"It is plain that Jesus is not God Himself" (Rev. Moon, *Divine Principle*, p. 258).

"But after his crucifixion, Christianity made Jesus into God. This is why a gap between God and man has never been bridged. Jesus is a man in whom God is incarnate, but he is not God Himself" (Rev. Moon, *Christianity in Crisis*, pp. 12, 13).

Moon tells his followers that they can not only equal Jesus, they can also excel Him.

"You can compare yourself with Jesus Christ, and feel you can be greater than Jesus Himself" (Sun Myung Moon, "The Way" translated by Won Pok Choi, from the *Master Speaks*, June 30, 1974, p. 4).

Jesus, according to Moon, was a failure: "Abraham was the father of faith, Moses was a man of faith, Jesus was the Son of man, trying to carry out his mission at the cost of his life. But they are, in a way, failures" (Sun Myung Moon, "Victory or Defeat," translated by Won Pok Choi, from *Master Speaks*, March 31, 1973, p. 1).

Speaking of the work of Christ, the writer to the Hebrews said, "For by one offering He has perfected for all time those who are sanctified" (Hebrews 10:14). The Scriptures testify that the work of Christ on the cross is complete, sufficient to secure the salvation of the individual. Jesus accomplished all that was necessary for the full salvation of mankind. He was not a failure.

The Death of Christ

The Bible plainly states that Jesus Christ came to this earth for the specific purpose of dying for the sins of the world, "Just as the Son of Man did not come to be served, but to serve, and to give His life a ransom for many" (Matthew 20:28).

Rev. Moon, however, teaches to the contrary: "We, therefore, must realize that Jesus did not come to die on the cross" (Rev. Moon, *Divine Principle*, p. 178).

The Scriptures teach "that God was in Christ reconciling the world to Himself" (II Corinthians 5:19). But Moon declares, ". . . the physical body of Jesus was invaded by Satan through the cross" (Rev. Moon, *Divine Principle*, p. 438).

Moon also thinks that the death of Christ was a victory for Satan: "Satan thus attained what he had intended through the 4,000-year course of history, by crucifying Jesus, with the exercise of his maximum power" (Rev. Moon, *Divine Principle*, p. 435).

He also teaches Christ's death was without effect: "It is equally true that the cross has been unable to establish the Kingdom of Heaven on Earth by removing our original sin" (Rev. Moon, *Divine Principle*, p. 178).

Moon, the Messiah?

As previously noted, Moon believes himself to be the person to finish the task left uncompleted by Jesus. The failure of Jesus leaves the way open for Moon. The *Divine Principle* states that the Messiah, the Lord of the Second Advent, must be born physically on earth to accomplish man's physical salvation. While neither the *Divine Principle* nor Moon publicly declare that he is the Messiah, the inference is strongly given that Moon is indeed the Lord of the Second Advent.

To his followers there appears to be no question about it; Moon is the Messiah. He is reportedly worshipped by his followers and given the designation "Father." Moon has stated, "God is now throwing Christianity away and is now establishing a new religion, and this new religion is the Unification Church" (*Time Magazine*, September 30, 1974).

The Bible portrays two comings of the Messiah. The first coming was fulfilled when Jesus of Nazareth was born to the virgin Mary. "Now after Jesus was born in Bethlehem of Judea in the days of Herod the King, behold, Magi, from the east arrived in Jerusalem, saying, 'Where is He who has been born King of the Jews?'" (Matthew 2:1, 2 NASB).

The Bible speaks over and over again of the second coming of Christ which will be a visible, bodily, return from Heaven."...Men of Galilee, why do you stand looking into the sky? This Jesus, who has been taken up from you into heaven, will come in just the same way as you have watched Him go into heaven" (Acts 1:11 NASB). "Behold, He is coming with the clouds, and every eye will see Him..." (Revelation 1:7 NASB).

There is no biblical teaching that the Messiah will be born physically a second time to accomplish any physical salvation. Jesus accomplished both physical and spiritual salvation at His first coming by His work on the cross. He is the only Savior. There is no need for another Messiah. "And there is salvation in no one else; for there is no other name under heaven that has been given among men, by which we must be saved" (Acts 4:12 NASB). Another Messiah is both unbiblical and unnecessary.

Conclusion

Although the Unification Church makes astounding claims for itself, the facts speak otherwise. The teaching of the *Divine Principle* is at odds with the Bible at all of its central points and therefore cannot be a completion of God's revelation. Moon has no messianic credentials and must be considered as a false prophet, of which Jesus warned us: "Beware of false prophets, who come to you in sheep's clothing, but inwardly are ravenous wolves. You will know them by their fruits" (Matthew 7:15, 16 NASB).

Unification Church Terms

Unification Church—Eastern cult founded by Korean Sun Myung Moon. Claims to have the complete truth of God which has just now been revealed to this present age through Moon. Considers its leader, Rev. Moon, the Messiah who is completing the salvation work unfinished by Jesus Christ.

Collegiate Association for the Research of Principles (CARP) — Front organization for the Unification Church, used to recruit members and funds from college areas.

Holy Spirit Association for the Unification of World Christianity — The complete name of the Unification Church.

Lord of the Second Advent — Title of the second Messiah, said to be Sun Myung Moon, who comes to complete the unfinished salvation work of Jesus Christ.

Master Speaks — Tapes and transcriptions of Moon's messages to his followers.

Moon, Sun Myung — Founder of the Unification Church. Born in Korea in 1920. Moon claims to have had a vision of Christ in 1936 in which he was told that he must finish the work which Christ began. His followers believe him to be the Messiah, the Lord of the Second Advent.

Moonies — Nickname (which they do not appreciate) for followers of Rev. Sun Myung Moon and the Unification Church.

New Hope Singers International — Singing publicity front organization for the Unification Church.

The Divine Principle — According to the Unification Church, the Divine Principle book is the completed testament, superseding the Bible, containing the present spiritual truth for this age which heretofore had not been revealed. Its author is the cult's founder and leader, Sun Myung Moon.

True Father and True Mother — Titles of Moon and his wife, ascribed to them by their followers in the Unification Church.

CHAPTER TWELVE

The Way International

History

The Way International, headquartered in New Knoxville, Ohio, was founded by Victor Paul Wierwille, a former Evangelical and Reformed minister. Wierwille was a pastor for some 16 years in northwestern Ohio when he resigned his pastorate and began teaching his own unique cult of Christianity. Disillusioned with orthodox biblical interpretation, he disposed of his library of some 3,000 volumes and began his own personal study of the Bible.

This culminated in his work, *Power for Abundant Living* (commonly seen on bumper stickers as PFAL), and around 1958, The Way International began. Membership today in The Way International can only be estimated since no official figures are released. The best estimates put it at about 50,000 active members

Claims of The Way International

Victor Paul Wierwille claims he had a so-called encounter with God:

> God spoke to me audibly, just like I'm talking to you now. He said he would teach me the word as it had not been known since the first century, if I would teach it to others (Elena S. Whiteside, *The Way: Living in Love*, New Knoxville, Ohio: American Christian Press, p. 178).

The inference from this is clear. God spoke to Wierwille

and told him that *no one* since the first century has been teaching the Bible accurately but now if he (Wierwille) would teach it to others, God would reveal to him the way it should be taught. The logical conclusion to this claim is that anyone who teaches or who has taught contrary to Wierwille is teaching something wrong.

The Way Magazine states, "The so-called Christian Church today is built essentially on man-made doctrine, tradition, confusion, bondage trips, and contradiction to the word as it was originally God-breathed" (*The Way Magazine*, September-October 1974, p. 7).

The Way International believes Victor Paul Wierwille has the only true interpretation of the Scriptures, and is the only one who can lead fellow Bible students out of the confusion in which traditional Christianity has engulfed them. This exclusive claim to inspiration is a characteristic of cults.

What is The Way International?

In a pamphlet entitled "This is the Way," the following explanation is given:

> The Way International is a biblical research and teaching organization concerned with setting before men and women of all ages the inherent accuracy of the word of God (the Bible) so that everyone who so desires may know the power of God in his life. The Way is not a church, nor is it a denomination or a religious sect of any sort (*This is the Way*, New Knoxville, Ohio: The Way International, n.d.).

Contrary to its lofty claims, The Way International is a non-Christian cult, characterized by the twisting and perverting of Holy Scripture by its founder, Victor Paul Wierwille.

Source of Authority

Although The Way strongly asserts that the Bible is its only recognized source of authority, in actuality it is the peculiar interpretation of the Bible by Wierwille that is its yardstick for truth. For all intents and purposes, The Way International has a second source of authority in forming its beliefs: Wierwille's writings and teachings.

According to Wierwille and The Way International, the

Bible does not teach that Jesus Christ is God. In 1975, Wierwille wrote a book titled *Jesus Christ Is Not God*, in which he stated, "If Jesus Christ is God and not the Son of God, we have not yet been redeemed" (p. 6).

In another work he had this to say, "God is eternal whereas Jesus was born...Jesus Christ's existence began when he was conceived by God's creating the soul-life of Jesus in Mary. God created, brought into existence, this life in an ovum in Mary's womb" (Victor Paul Wierwille, *The Word's Way*, Vol. 3, pp. 26, 37).

Wierwille further states: "Those who teach that Jesus Christ is God and God is Jesus Christ will never stand approved in 'rightly dividing' God's word, for there is only one God, and 'Thou shalt have no other gods'."

"The Bible clearly teaches that Jesus Christ was a man conceived by the Holy Spirit, God, whose life was without blemish and without spot, a lamb from the flock, thereby being the perfect sacrifice. Thus he became our redeemer" (Victor Paul Wierwille, *Jesus Christ is Not God*, p. 79).

"If the Bible had taught that there is a Christian trinity, I would have happily accepted it. (Victor Paul Wierwille, ibid., p. 3).

Wierwille's view of the Bible is different from the historic view of the Church. He says, "...The records in the gospels are addressed at times to Israel and at other times to the Gentiles, but never to the Church of God. One of the greatest errors in the translations of the Bible was placing the four gospels in the New Testament. The gospels logically belong in the Old Testament" (Victor Paul Wierwille, *Power for Abundant Living*, New Knoxville, Ohio: American Christian Press, 1980, p.5).

However, the rearrangement of the four gospels is not the only manipulating that Wierwille does with the Bible. As the Passantinos point out,

"...Wierwille claims that he properly interprets the Bible and preserves the meaning of the text, confident that it is God's infallible Word. But in practice, he manipulates texts, adds words to them in brackets, and, if all else fails, claims that the original meaning was "lost" by the Apostate Church and that God has given it especially to him to reveal to the world. Such practices effectively make the Bible little more than a tool in Wierwille's work to build his own system (Robert and Gretchen Passantino, *Answers to the Cultist at Your Door*, Eugene Oregon: Harvest House Publishers, 1981 p. 166).

Danny Frigulti, who has done an extensive study and exposé of The Way, points out a few of the areas of Wierwille's poor research:

Wierwille: "Tertullian (early third century; the first person to use the word trinity of the Father, Son and Holy Spirit)".

The truth: Tertullian (160-220) was not the first person to use the word "Trinity". Theophilus (116-168-181) used the word "Trinity" in this writing. "In like manner also the three days which were before the luminaries, are types of the *Trinity*, of God, and His Word, and His wisdom."

Wierwille: "The Greek Christian Justin Martyr who wrote in the middle of the second century *never* quoted in the name of the Father, and of the Son, and of the Holy Ghost."

The truth: "For, in the name of God, the Father and the Lord of the universe, and of our Savior Jesus Christ, and of the Holy Spirit, they then receive the washing with water." These are the words of Justin Martyr.

Wierwille: "The Nicene Creed embraced the Son as co-equal with God. Two hundred eighteen of the 220 bishops signed this creed."

The truth: Approximately 318 bishops were present at the Council of Nicea, along with 1500 other bishops, elders and deacons.

Wierwille: "Thus the usage of God in Hebrews 1:8 shows Jesus Christ in an exalted position; he is, however, not God the Creator."

The truth: Chapter six shows that Jesus is God the Creator.

Wierwille: "The man worshipped him according to verse 38, not because he was God the Creator, but because he was a religious man superior to himself."

The truth: Jesus receives this worship, and the Greek word for worship in this verse (John 9:38) is the same that is given to God alone. Therefore, Jesus is God.

Wierwille: "He was not the alpha as God is the Alpha and Omega."

The truth: Jesus in Revelation 1:8, 11 and 22:13 declares that *He is* the Alpha and Omega. Therefore, He is from beginning to end.

To substantiate his claim that Christ is not God, Wierwille contends that the deity of Christ (as expressed in the Trinity) is not part of Christian teaching or writing in the first three centuries after Christ (Victor Paul Wierwille, *Jesus Christ is Not God*, p. 12). This dogmatic statement only reveals the shallowness of Wierwille's scholarship.

Ignatius, (A.D. 50-115), an early Church Father and disciple of the Apostle John, *clearly* writes of Christ's deity. Irenaeus (A.D. 115-190), another Church Father, makes clear reference in *Against Heresies* X. 1 when he calls Christ Jesus Lord and God. The apologist Tertullian (A.D. 160-220) calls Christ the God of God. Also Hippolytus, Origen and Lucian of Antioch, all clearly refer to Christ as the one God.

One of the strongest arguments for deity is worship. The very word worship connotes divinity. Wierwille himself states," There has always been one sin which God did not and will not tolerate and that is worshipping any god other than God the Creator."

Here Wierwille is in agreement with Scripture, "Worship the Lord your God and serve Him only." The Old Testament reference is Deuteronomy 6:10 and Exodus 20:2-6. What is found in the New Testament is that Jesus Christ clearly receives worship, and approves of homage paid to him.

In Matt. 14:22-33, Christ clearly accepts the disciples' worship, after the storm. The blind man in John 9 worships Christ. The triumphal entry in the gospels is one of the clearest examples of Christ receiving worship, yet is often overlooked. God the Father commands us to worship the son in Hebrews 1:6. In all these passages the same word for worship is used.

The Trinity

Wierwille, like many other cultists, holds a unitarian view of God (that God is one person, not three). Consequently, he rejects the doctrine of the Trinity. "Long before the founding of Christianity the idea of a triune god or a god-in-three-persons was a common belief in ancient religions. Although many of these religions had many minor deities, they distinctly acknowledge that there was one supreme God who consisted of three persons or essences. The Babylonians used an equilateral triangle to represent this three-in-one-god, now the symbol of the modern three-in-one believers." Although the charge that the Trinity is pagan in origin is frequently brought up by cultists, it has no basis in fact. Any so-called parallel between the Trinity and pagan views of the nature of God do not exist. Any comparison will reveal the vast difference between the two.

"Trinitarian dogma degrades God from his elevated unparalleled position, besides it leaves man unredeemed."

The problem with Wierwille's position is that he misunderstands the doctrine of the Holy Trinity. Simply stated, there is one God and this one God is three distinct persons, the Father, the Son, and the Holy Spirit, and these three persons are equal to the one God. We do not believe in three gods but rather one God who is three persons. It is the clear teaching of Scripture and the historic belief of the Christian Church.

The Scriptures teach there is only one God, "For there is one God, and one mediator also between God and men, the man Christ Jesus" (1 Timothy 2:5 NASB). The Scriptures also teach that there is a person called the Father who is designated God, "Paul, an apostle (not sent from men, nor through the agency of man, but through Jesus Christ, and God the Father, who raised him from the dead" (Galatians 1:1 NASB).

The Bible speaks of a second person, called the Son, who is personally different from the Father but who is also called God: "In the beginning was the Word and the Word was with God and the Word was God...and the Word became flesh, and dwelt among us" (John 1:1, 14 NASB). "For this cause therefore the Jews were seeking all the more to kill Him, because He not only was breaking the Sabbath, but also was calling God His own Father, making Himself equal with God" (John 5:18 NASB).

Moreover the Bible talks about a third person who is distinct from both the Father and the Son who is also called God. "But Peter said, 'Ananias, why has Satan filled your heart to lie to the Holy Spirit...you have not lied to men, but to God'" (Acts 5:3, 4 NASB).

Thus the Father is called God, the Son is also referred to as God and the Holy Spirit is called God. The Bible clearly teaches that only one God exists. Therefore, the Father, the Son and the Holy Spirit are equal to the one God. This is the biblical doctrine of the Trinity.

Additional support for the Trinity comes from the choice of words in the Old Testament. In the famous Jewish *Shema* of Deuteronomy 6:4, the backbone of historic Judaic teaching, it reads, "Hear, O Israel! The Lord is our God, the Lord is one."

The passage says, "God is one." But what does this mean? The word for "one" here is *echod*, the exact same word used for "one" in Genesis 1:5 where it reads, "The evening and the morning were the first day." Also the same as the word "one" in Genesis 2:24, "They shall become one flesh."

All of these usages refer to a plurality. There is light and darkness in the one day. There is husband and wife in one flesh. "Here *echod* is used to show oneness in a compound sense."

The power of this argument is driven home by Hebrews where there is a word for perfect unity or oneness. The word is *yachid*. It is often translated as "only." The word can be found in Genesis 22:2, Judges 11:34 and Jeremiah 6:26.

Virgin Birth

Wierwille also denies that Jesus of Nazareth was virgin born.

> If it said a virgin shall bring forth a son your Bible would fall to pieces. It says plainly that Mary was a virgin only at the time of conception, not at Jesus' birth; the theory of virgin birth has been a theological assumption and erroneous teaching. The Bible said in verse 20 that God told Joseph, "Take unto thee thy wife" when Joseph took her unto himself he lived with her as a husband lives with a wife. She was a virgin when she conceived by God, but when Joseph took her unto himself she was no longer a virgin. The divine conception made Mary no longer a virgin (*The Way Magazine,* Dec. 1970, p. 6).

His contention is refuted by Matthew: "Behold, the virgin shall be with child, and shall bear a son, and they shall call his name Immanuel which translated means, 'God with us'. And Joseph arose from his sleep, and did as the angel of the Lord commanded him, and took her as his wife, and kept her a virgin until she gave birth to a son; and he called His name Jesus" (Matthew 1:23-25 NASB).

Salvation

Wierwille believes salvation is manifest not only by believing in Christ but also by speaking in tongues.

> ...the only visible and audible proof that a man has been born again and filled with the gift from the Holy Spirit is *always* that he speaks in a tongue or tongues (Victor Paul Wierwille, *Receiving the Holy Spirit Today*, p. 148).

Thus, according to Wierwille, there must be a verbal confession of faith in Christ followed by the proof of speaking in tongues. However, the Scriptures attest that simple belief in Jesus Christ is sufficient for salvation. "He that believeth on the Son hath everlasting life" (John 3:36).

Wierwille also teaches the unbiblical doctrine that salvation includes physical wholeness in this life. "When we have salvation, we have wholeness, even physical wholeness, if we simply accept it" (Victor Paul Wierwille, *The New Dynamic Church*, Studies in Abundant Living, Vol. #2, p. 31). The Bible teaches that we will have physical wholeness but only at the resurrection of the dead. "So also is the resurrection of the dead. It is sown a perishable body, it is raised an imperishable body" (1 Corinthians 15:42 NASB).

The Way's doctrine of salvation is unscriptural in its advocating the visible sign of speaking in tongues. Salvation is a free gift from God given to all those who put their faith in Christ. There is never any hint in Scripture that it is authenticated by speaking in tongues. Furthermore, the basis of The Way's doctrine of salvation is an erroneous view of the person of Jesus Christ.

Wierwille also teaches a sinless perfection doctrine that says after a person is converted his spirit can never sin: "...Do we sin in the spirit? No, but in body and soul we fall" (Victor Paul Wierwille, *Power for Abundant Living*, p. 313).

But the apostle John said, speaking to the believer, "If we say we have no sin, we are deceiving ourselves, and the truth is not in us....If we say that we have not sinned, we make Him a liar, and His word is not in us" (1 John 1:8, 10 NASB). Until the believer is changed from corruptible to incorruptible he will keep on sinning.

Holy Spirit vs. holy spirit

According to biblical teaching, the Holy Spirit is one of the Godhead, the third person of the Holy Trinity. According to Victor Paul Wierwille, there is Holy Spirit (which is the same as God the Father) and holy spirit, uncapitalized (which is God's gift to man). Wierwille has said, "The giver is God the Spirit. His gift is spirit. Failure to recognize the difference between the giver and His gift has caused no end of confusion in the Holy Spirit field of study" (Victor Paul Wierwille, *Receiving the Holy Spirit Today*, p. 3).

However, it is Wierwille who is confused on the subject for the Scriptures do not make the distinction he claims. In Matthew 28:19 (NASB) Jesus exhorts believers to baptize "in the name of the Father and the Son and the Holy Spirit." This demonstrates that the Father and the Holy Spirit are two distinct persons, not one and the same.

Another example of the distinction between the Father and the Holy Spirit can be found in the account in Luke of the baptism of Jesus. "Now it came about when all the people were baptized, that Jesus also was baptized, and while He was praying, heaven was opened and the Holy Spirit descended upon Him in bodily form like a dove, and a voice came out of heaven. 'Thou art my beloved son, in Thee I am well pleased' " (Luke 3:21, 22 NASB).

Wierwille's identification of the Father with the Holy Spirit is incorrect and his uncapitalizing holy spirit on certain occasions in order to demonstrate a difference between the gift and the giver is arbitrary and cannot be justified.

Abundant Life

The following is taken from a poster that can be seen on numerous college campuses announcing the Power for Abundant Living Course that The Way International uses to induct one into its teachings and practices:

YOU CAN HAVE POWER FOR ABUNDANT LIVING

Abundant living means you can be SET FREE from all fear; doubt and bondage; DELIVERED from poverty, sickness and poor health; OVERFLOWING with life, vitality and zest; RESCUED from condemnation and self-contempt; CURED of drugs and sex abuse. You can RESTORE your broken marriage; ENJOY a happy united family, where there is no generation gap.

If you have power for abundant living you can GAIN self-respect; enjoy SATISFYING work with more than ADEQUATE income. You can OVERCOME depression, discouragement and disappointment and have LOVE, JOY AND REAL PEACE. There can always be a POSITIVE outlook on life, day after day, with no let down. There can be a new PURPOSE in your life. If you have the more abundant life.

YOU CAN HAVE WHATEVER YOU WANT!

Every problem you ever had can be overcome when you are fully and accurately instructed.

The claims are monumental: deliverance from doubt, poverty, sickness, overflowing with vitality, having a happy satisfied life; who would not want this?

The Deity of Jesus Christ

The central issue of Christianity as related to the cults is the divinity of Jesus Christ. Many teachings of the cults are similar to orthodox Christianity, but concerning the deity of Christ they never agree. No cult regards Christ as God come in the flesh.

The deity is considered here as a separate issue from the closely related teaching of the Trinity. The reason for this is due to the many critical implications if Jesus is not actually God's Son. Christ promises freedom, forgiveness, eternal life, all of which He makes dependent on His identity as God.

If a comparison is made between the attributes and titles attributed to God and those attributed to Christ, one is left with no choice but to conclude that Jesus is God. This is only one of many avenues of proof, but it is overwhelming in its impact.

Attributes of God	the Father	and the Son
1. from everlasting	Psalm 90:2	Micah 5:2
2. first and last	Isiah 44:6	Revelation 1:17
3. fills all	Jeremiah 23:24	Ephesians 4:10
4. does not change	Malachi 3:6	Hebrews 13:8
5. is the Almighty	Exodus 6:3	Revelation 1:8
6. God of truth	Deuteronomy 32:4	John 14:6
7. creates all things	Isaiah 44:24	Colossians 1:16
8. King of Kings	1 Timothy 6:15	Revelation 19:16
9. everlasting dominion	Psalm 145:13	Daniel 7:14
10. final Judge	Romans 14:10	2 Corinthians 5:10
11. name is above all	Psalm 83:18	Philippians 2:9
12. reward is with Him	Isaiah 40:10	Revelation 22:12
13. perfect love	1 John 4:8	John 15:9
14. the light	1 John 1:5	John 1:5-9; 8:12
15. our hope	Psalm 39:7	Titus 2:13
16. takes away death	Isaiah 25:8	2 Timothy 1:10
17. every knee bows	Isaiah 45:23	Philippians 2:10
18. blots out sin	Isaiah 43:25	1 John 1:7
19. forgives sin	Exodus 34:7	Mark 2:5
20. calms sea	Psalm 107:29	Matthew 8:26
21. prepares heavenly city	Hebrews 11:16	John 14:2
22. glorify His name	Isaiah 24:15	2 Thessalonians 1:12
23. glory forever	Galatians 1:4, 5	2 Peter 3:18

Conclusion

Victor Paul Wierwille's claim that he is teaching the Scriptures as they had not been known since the first century is a distortion of the facts. Wierwille's teachings are authoritarian and are at odds with Holy Scripture. The teachings deny basic Christian beliefs, such as the doctrine of Jesus Christ, the virgin birth, the Holy Spirit, the Trinity and salvation. The inescapable conclusion is that

The Way International is a non-Christian cult and must be treated as such.

The Way International Terms

The Way International—Contemporary American cult founded by Victor Paul Wierwille with headquarters in New Knoxville, Ohio. Denies the deity of Christ, personality and deity of the Holy Spirit. The Way also teaches a salvation by works. They sell a Power for Abundant Living course advertising the ability to solve life's problems by following their system.

The American Christian Press—The publishing arm of The Way International cult.

Lamsa, George—Aramaic teacher for The Way International cult. He erroneously teaches that the New Testament was originally written in Aramaic instead of Greek.

Power for Abundant Living—Title of The Way International introductory course designed to induct one into the teachings and practices of the cult.

The Rock of Ages—Annual convention of The Way International cult, held in New Knoxville, Ohio.

Wierwille, Victor Paul—Former minister in the Evangelical and Reformed Church who became dissatisfied with the way the church interpreted the Bible. Throwing away his entire theological library of over 3,000 volumes, he began his own study of the Bible. Claiming to have heard an audible voice from God informing him that he (Wierwille) would now teach the Bible like it had not been taught since the first century, Wierwille proceeded to found the cult called The Way International.

WOW Ambassadors—Volunteer missionaries of The Way International. WOW stands for "The Word Over the World."

CHAPTER THIRTEEN

The Worldwide Church of God "Armstrongism"

History

The founder of the Worldwide Church of God is Herbert W. Armstrong, born on July 31, 1892 in Des Moines, Iowa. As a young man, Armstrong worked in the advertising business and showed little interest in spiritual things. In a dispute with his wife over the issue of keeping the seventh-day Sabbath, Armstrong began an intensive personal study of the Bible. This resulted in his agreeing with his wife on observing the Saturday Sabbath. Further Bible study convinced Armstrong that much of what he had been taught in traditional churches was wrong.

> ...I found that the popular church teachings and practices were not based on the Bible. They had originated, as research in history had revealed, in paganism. Numerous Bible prophecies foretold it; the amazing unbelievable truth was, the SOURCE of these popular beliefs and practices of professing Christianity, was quite largely paganism, and human reasoning and custom, NOT the Bible! (Herbert W. Armstrong, *The Autobiography of Herbert W. Armstrong*, Pasadena: Ambassador College Press, 1967, pp. 298, 299).

According to Armstrong, the Worldwide Church of God began in January, 1934 when the "Sardis" era of the church ended and the "Philadelphia" era began (a reference to the seven churches listed in Revelation two and three that some see as a prefiguring of eras of church history). Armstrong put it this way:

...back in 1934...Jesus Christ (Rev. 3:8) was opening the gigantic mass media DOOR of radio and the printing press for the proclamation of His same original GOSPEL to all the world! (Ibid., p. 503).

Armstrong at this time began his radio braodcast and the publishing of the magazine *The Plain Truth*. Since its inception, the Worldwide Church of God has experienced significant growth reaching into millions of homes through the distribution of its magazine and the World Tomorrow radio broadcast.

Garner Ted Armstrong

An important figure in the Worldwide Church of God was Herbert W. Armstrong's fourth child, Garner Ted. Rejecting his father's religion, Garner Ted wanted to be a television or movie star but certain crises in his life led him to study the Bible and then concur with his father's teachings.

Garner Ted became the national broadcaster of the Worldwide Church of God, the Vice-Chancellor of Ambassador College in Pasadena, California, and the Vice-President of the Worldwide Church of God. However, in 1972, Garner Ted fell out of favor with his father and for a short period was relieved of his responsibilities. A few months later, his responsibilities were restored.

More recently however, Garner Ted was expelled from his father's church. Not to be outdone, Garner Ted formed his own offshoot, the Church of God International, headquartered in Tyler, Texas. The reason for his dismissal was a charge of alleged immoral conduct.

The Claims of Armstrong

Herbert W. Armstrong makes no small claim for his work in the Worldwide Church of God. "...A.D. 69, the apostles and the church fled to Pella from Jerusalem according to Jesus' warning (Matthew 24:15, 16). That was the END of the organized proclaiming of Christ's gospel by His church to the world!...For eighteen and one-half centuries, all worldwide organized proclaiming of Christ's gospel was stamped out..." (Ibid., pp. 502, 503).

I'm going to give you the frank and straightforward answer.

You have a right to know all about this great work of God, and about me. First, let me say—this may sound incredible, but it's true—Jesus Christ foretold this very work—it is, itself the fulfillment of his prophecy (Matthew 24:14 and Mark 13:10).

Astounding as it may seem, there is no other work on earth proclaiming to the whole world this very same gospel that Jesus taught and proclaimed!

And listen again! Read this twice! Realize this, incredible though it may seem—no other work on earth is proclaiming this true gospel of Christ to the whole world as Jesus foretold in Matthew 24:14 and Mark 13:10! This is the most important activity on earth today! (Herbert W. Armstrong, Personal letter to Robert Sumner, November 27, 1958, cited by Walter Martin, *The Rise of The Cults*, Santa Ana, California: Vision House Publishers, Revised ed. 1977, pp. 35, 36).

Armstrong believes his work of restoring the lost gospel is preparatory to the second coming of Christ: "For eighteen and one-half centuries that gospel was not preached. The world was deceived into accepting a false gospel. Today Christ has raised up his work and once again allotted two nineteen-year time cycles for proclaiming His same gospel, preparatory to His second coming." He also states:

"No man ever spoke like this man," reported the officers of the Pharisees regarding Jesus. The multitudes were astonished at his doctrine.

It is the same today, the same living Christ through The World Tomorrow broadcast, The Plain Truth Magazine, and this work proclaims in mighty power around the world the same gospel preached by Peter, Paul and all the original apostles...The World Tomorrow and The Plain Truth are Christ's instruments which he is powerfully using. Yes, His message is shocking today. Once again it is the voice in the wilderness of religious confusion (*The Inside Story of The World Tomorrow Broadcast*, pp. 2, 7).

The Worldwide Church of God considers Herbert W. Armstrong as the man God chose to bring the truth to this present age: "Jesus chose Paul, who was highly educated for spreading the gospel to the Gentiles. He later raised up Peter Waldo, a successful businessman, to keep his truth alive during the middle ages. In these last days WHEN

156

THE GOSPEL MUST GO AROUND THE WORLD, Jesus chose a man amply trained in the advertising and business fields to shoulder the mission—Herbert W. Armstrong; (Herman Hoeh, *A True History of the Church*, p. 28).

The lines are clearly drawn. If you do not believe the message of Herbert W. Armstrong and the Worldwide Church of God then you do not believe the true message of Christ to this age.

God

Like the Mormons, Armstrong believes in a plurality of personal gods, based upon the Hebrew word for God, "Elohim."

"And as I have explained previously, God is not a single person, but the Hebrew word for God portrays God as a FAMILY of persons" (Herbert W. Armstrong, "What is the True Gospel?," *Tomorrow's World*, January, 1970, p. 7). "Elohim is a uniplural or collective noun, such as "church" or "family" or "kingdom." In other words, Elohim stands for a single class composed of TWO or MORE individuals. Elohim, then, is the "God Kingdom" or "God Family" (Herbert W. Armstrong, ed. *Ambassador College Correspondence Course*, 1972, Lesson 8, p. 5).

The Trinity

There is no biblical Trinity in Armstrong's theology. Presently the Godhead is limited to the Father and the Son but in the future more persons will be added to the Godhead. "God is a family—not a trinity. God's family will not be limited to an intractably closed circle of three...God's family is open" (B. McDowell, "Is the Holy Spirit a Person?," *Tomorrow's World*, September 1970, p. 31).

Armstrong feels that the doctrine of the Trinity is the result of the teaching of false prophets: "...the theologians and 'higher critics' have blindly accepted the heretical and false doctrine introduced by pagan false prophets who crept in, that the Holy Spirit is a third person—the heresy of the 'trinity.' This limits God to 'three persons.'" (Herbert W. Armstrong, *Just What Do You Mean—Born Again*, p. 19).

THE WORLDWIDE CHURCH OF GOD/"ARMSTRONGISM" 157

The accusations leveled by Armstrong against the doctrine of the Trinity are unfounded. Rather than being the invention of false prophets and heretics, the doctrine of the Trinity is the clear teaching of Scripture on the nature of God. Simply stated, the Bible teaches there exists one God who is three separate persons: the Father, the Son, and the Holy Spirit, and these three persons are the one God. There is no teaching whatever in Scripture that suggests God is a family.

The Holy Spirit

Herbert W. Armstrong and his followers reject the personality and deity of the Holy Spirit. "...the Holy Spirit is not a person but the power God the Father uses— much as a man uses electricity" (B. McDowell, op. cit., p. 32). "God's spirit is His mind, His power, His very essence, but it is not a distinct person as is the Father or Christ" (David John Hill, "Why is God the Father Called a Father?" *Tomorrow's World*, September 1970, p. 28.) "God's spirit, which is not a person, but the power of God..." (G. Geis, "The God Family: Open or Closed?," *Tomorrow's World*, September 1970, p. 30).

The views of Armstrongism concerning the Holy Spirit fly right into the face of true biblical teaching. The Bible clearly portrays the Holy Spirit as being deity, having a separate personality from both the Father and the Son.

This can be observed in Acts 5:3, 4 (NASB), where the Holy Spirit is spoken of as God, "But Peter said, 'Ananias, why has Satan filled your heart to lie to the Holy Spirit...You have not lied to men but to God.'"

Man

The final destiny of man is to become God: "You are setting out on a training to become creator—to become God!" (Herbert W. Armstrong, *Why Were You Born*, op. cit., p. 22). "...we develop spiritually ready to be finally BORN OF GOD—by a resurrection, or instantaneous conversion from mortal to immortal, from human to divine..." (David Hill and Robert Kuhn, "Why Does God Hide Himself?," *Tomorrow's World*, 1969, p. 34).

"The PURPOSE OF LIFE is that in us God is really

recreating His own kind—reproducing Himself after His own kind—for we are, upon real conversion, actually begotten as sons (yet unborn) of God...we grow spiritually more and more like God, until, at the time of the resurrection we shall be instantaneously changed from mortal to immortal—we shall be born of God—WE SHALL THEN BE GOD!" (David Jon Hill, op. cit., p. 27).

The idea that man will some day be God can be found nowhere in the Bible. God is God by nature. He was, is and always will be God. Man cannot attain Godhood for he is finite, limited by his nature. There is no other God neither will there be any other God: " 'You are my witnesses,' declares the Lord, 'and my servant whom I have chosen, in order that you may know and believe me and understand that I am He. Before Me there was no God formed, and there will be none after me' "(Isaiah 43:10 NASB).

Salvation by Works

As is the case with all non-Christian cults, Armstrongism teaches that salvation is achieved by the individual's self-effort rather than relying only on God's grace.

"Salvation, then is a process! But how the God of this world would blind your eyes to that!!! He tries to deceive you into thinking all there is to it is just 'accepting Christ' with 'no works'—and presto-change, you are pronounced 'saved.' But the Bible reveals that none is yet 'saved' " (Herbert W. Armstrong, *Why Were You Born?*, p. 11).

According to the Worldwide Church of God, salvation is a process beginning in this life and culminating in the resurrection. Salvation consists of repentance, faith and water baptism. No one is saved in this life. The doctrine of "simply" coming to Christ for salvation is rejected by Armstrong in the strongest of terms.

People have been taught, falsely, that "Christ completed the plan of salvation on the cross"—when actually it was only begun there. The popular denominations have taught "just believe, that's all there is to it; believe on the Lord Jesus Christ, and you are that instant saved!" That teaching is false! And because of deception, because the true gospel of Jesus Christ has been blotted out, lo these 1900 years by the preaching of a false gospel about the person of Christ—and often a false Christ at that—millions today worship Christ—and all in vain! (Herbert W. Armstrong, *All About Water Baptism*, p. 1).

According to Armstrong, a person must be baptized in order to be saved "...God commands water baptism; and for one who is able to either defy the command and refuse, or neglect...certainly would be an act of disobedience which would impose the PENALTY of sin, and cause loss of salvation" (Ibid., p. 19).

Moreover, the Saturday Sabbath needs to be observed to attain salvation: "Thus did God reveal which day is HIS SABBATH, and also that it DOES MAKE LIFE-AND-DEATH DIFFERENCE—for to break God's Holy Sabbath is SIN, and the penalty is eternal DEATH" (Herbert W. Armstrong, *Which Day is the Christian Sabbath?*, Pasadena: Ambassador College Press, 1971, p. 35).

Contrary to Armstrong's statements, the Scriptures teach that salvation is a free gift from God. The Scriptures further declare that salvation cannot be earned by doing any work, whether it be water baptism or the keeping of the Sabbath. Salvation comes as a result of a person simply placing his faith in Jesus Christ:

"For by grace you have been saved through faith; and that not of yourselves, it is the gift of God; not as a result of works, that no one should boast" (Ephesians 2:8, 9 NASB). "He saved us, not on the basis of deeds which we have done in righteousness, but according to His mercy, by the washing of regeneration and renewing by the Holy Spirit" (Titus 3:5 NASB).

Salvation, therefore, is totally a work of God. Man can add nothing to what Christ has already done when He died in our place on the cross.

Eternal Judgment

Armstrong rejects any idea of eternal punishment for the wicked. "The wages of sin is death" (Romans 6:23) and the death, which is the absence of life, is for ALL ETERNITY. It is eternal punishment by remaining DEAD for all eternity—not remaining alive and being tortured in a fictitious, burning hell-fire!" (Herbert W. Armstrong, *"Immortality,"* p. 7).

The fires of hell spoken of in the Bible will eventually burn themselves out, he says: "They (the fires in the valley of Hinnom) were never quenched or put out by anyone! The flames merely died out when they had nothing more to consume. Even so, it will be with the Gehenna fire. It will be unquenched—but it will finally burn itself out" (Herbert W. Armstrong, ed., *Ambassador College Correspondence Course*, Lesson 6, p. 14).

The idea that hell will eventually burn itself out is not scriptural: "And these will go away into eternal punishment, but the righteous into eternal life" (Matthew 25:46). If there is no eternal punishment, then certainly there is no eternal life for this verse uses the same word to describe both. Jesus said the fire is unquenchable, "And if your eye causes you to stumble, cast it out; it is better for you to enter the Kingdom of God with one eye, than having two eyes to be cast into hell, where the *worm does not die, and the fire is not quenched*" (Mark 9:47, 48 NASB, italics ours).

The Sabbath

Armstrong believes observing Sunday as the day of worship is the Mark of the Beast: "Sunday observance—this is the Mark of the Beast...If in your forehead and your hand, you shall be tormented by God's plagues without mercy, yes, you!" (Herbert W. Armstrong, *The Mark of the Beast*, Pasadena: Ambassador College Press, 1957, pp. 10, 11).

Since there are other cultic groups which teach a similar doctrine about the Sabbath, we feel it necessary to demonstrate that it was the policy of the New Testament believers and the early church to observe Sunday rather than Saturday as their day of worship.

The teaching that the day of worship was changed from Saturday to Sunday during the reign of the Roman Emperor Constantine (c. A.D. 325) does not fit the facts. The fact that the early church believed the Hebrew Sabbath was not binding on the Christian is demonstrated by the following quotations:

At the beginning of the second century, Ignatius, bishop of Antioch, wrote to the Magnesians:

"Be not deceived with strange doctrines, nor with old fables.
For if we still live according to the Jewish law, we
acknowledge that we have not received grace"; and then goes
on to categorize his readers as "those who were brought up in
the ancient order of things" but who "have come to the
possession of a new hope, no longer observing the Sabbath"
(*The Ante-Nicene Fathers*, Vol. 1 pp. 62, 63).

During the middle of the second century, Justin Martyr
explained why Christians did not keep the law of Moses
and the Sabbath observance in *The Ante-Nicene Fathers*,
Vol. I, pp. 199, 200, 204, 207; and *Dialogue with Trypho*.

The same is true with Cerenalus, Bishop of Lyons at the
end of the second century (*Against Heresies*, Book IV,
chap. 16). Also Clement of Alexandria (*The Stromata*) and
Tertullian (*On Idolatry*, chap. 14 and *An Answer to the
Jew*, chap. 2), testify of the early Christians' attitude
concerning Sabbath observance. It was basically a Jewish
institution.

The New Birth

Armstrong and his followers have a peculiar view
regarding the new birth. They believe an individual is not
born of God until the resurrection. Rather, he is only
"begotten" (like pregnant) of God at his conversion:
"When we are converted, our sins forgiven, we receive the
Holy Spirit, we are then BEGOTTEN of God—not yet
BORN of God... Even as Christ was BORN AGAIN, born
of God by his resurrection, even so WE—the brethren—
shall be BORN AGAIN as sons of God, through the
RESURRECTION of the dead..." (Herbert W. Armstrong,
"Was Jesus Christ Born Again?" in *The Plain Truth*,
February 1963, p. 40).

Until now Christ is the only person who has been born
again. The rest of the believers must await a future
resurrection to experience the new birth.

Armstrongism is incorrect in this assertion. A person
becomes born again the moment he trusts Christ. The
Apostle Peter, while speaking to believers, said, "For you
have been born again not of seed which is perishable but
imperishable, that is, through the living and abiding word
of God" (I Peter 1:23 NASB, italics ours). Either St. Peter is
correct or Armstrong is correct. They cannot both be true

at the same time. Again, Armstrong's teachings are contradictory to Scripture.

False Prophecy

Armstrongism teaches that in A.D. 70 the true believers were scattered after completing two 19-year cycles of ministry to the world (A.D. 31 to A.D. 69). The church, at this time, departed from the faith. As God allowed the true believers in the first century to complete their two cycles of ministry, He also has decided to again allow the genuine believers to complete two more 19-year cycles.

The work began in 1934 and should have ended in 1972. Anticipating this, Herbert W. Armstrong made predictions concerning the United States and Great Britain as the year 1972 approached. In 1967 he wrote, "...we are to have soon (probably in about four years) such drought, and famine, that disease epidemics will follow, taking millions of lives... that condition is coming! And I do not mean in 400 years—nor in 40 years—but in the very next FOUR or FIVE" (Herbert W. Armstrong, *The United States and British Commonwealth in Prophecy*, p. 184).

Armstrong wrote concerning a great drought that was to strike the United States: "...it will strike sooner than 1975—probably between 1965 and 1972! This will be the very beginning as Jesus said, of the Great Tribulation" (Herbert W. Armstrong, *1975 in Prophecy*, Pasadena: Ambassador College Press, 1952, p. 10).

Interestingly enough, Armstrong has disqualified himself as a prophet, "Emphatically I am NOT a prophet, in the sense of one to whom God speaks specially and directly, revealing personally a future event to happen or new truth, or new and special instruction direct from God—separate from, and apart from what is contained in the Bible" (Herbert W. Armstrong, "Personal from Herbert W. Armstrong," *Tomorrow's World*, February, 1972, p. 1).

Even though Armstrong denies that he has been given a prophetic office, he nevertheless claims for himself to be God's messenger for this day and age, preaching the one true gospel. His false predictions demonstrate that he is not a true prophet of God and his claim as to being God's messenger is also untrue.

The Bible has harsh words to say for those who

prophesy falsely, "But the prophet who shall speak a word presumptuously in My name which I have not commanded him to speak...that prophet shall die" (Deuteronomy 18:20 NASB). The Scriptures indicate that to prophesy falsely in the name of the Lord is a serious offense.

Conclusion

"And there is only ONE CHURCH on earth today which understands and is proclaiming that exact order of events, doing the WORK of God in preaching His message to the world as a last witness" (Roderick Meredity, "The True Church—Where Is It?, *The Plain Truth*, March 1963, p. 44).

The two 19-year cycles have come and gone (1934-1972), Armstrong's work continues and Christ has not appeared again as He was supposed to appear. Further, there have been no great catastrophes to hit the United States and Great Britain as Armstrong predicted. These facts totally undermine the claim of Armstrong and his followers that the Worldwide Church of God is God's true church today.

Furthermore, the totally unbiblical doctrines about God being a family, salvation by works, the new birth not taking place until the resurrection, along with their other teachings, signify them to be a non-Christian cult that should be avoided.

The Worldwide Church of God Terms

The Worldwide Church of God (formerly the Radio Church of God) — Founded in 1934 by Herbert W. Armstrong, it teaches a mixture of British-Israelism, Seventh-day Adventism, Jehovah's Witnesses, and Armstrong's own unique interpretations about salvation and the nature of God.

Ambassador College — Liberal arts and religious college of the Worldwide Church of God.

Anglo-Israelism (British Israelism) — Identifies the ten tribes of Israel, which were supposedly lost, with the Anglo-Saxon nations. These nations, particularly the U.S. and Great Britain, and the events affecting them, are seen as being the fulfillment of all Bible prophecy concerning Israel. This doctrine is taught by Herbert W. Armstrong and his Worldwide Church of God.

Armstrong, Garner Ted—Son of Herbert W. Armstrong and former broadcaster for the Worldwide Church of God before his dismissal from the cult. Presently leads the Church of God International, a similar cult headquartered in Tyler, Texas.

Armstrong, Herbert W.—Born in Des Moines, Iowa in 1902. In 1934, he founded the Radio Church of God, now known as the Worldwide Church of God, an American-based cult.

Radio Church of God—Former name of the Worldwide Church of God.

The Plain Truth—Magazine of the Worldwide Church of God cult.

The World Tomorrow—Radio and television show of the Worldwide Church of God.

Tomorrow's World—Former magazine of the Worldwide Church of God.

CHAPTER FOURTEEN

Christian Science

History

The founder of Christian Science was Mary Ann Morse Baker Glover Patterson Eddy, born in Bow, New Hampshire in 1821, to Mark and Abigail Baker. Her parents were members of the Congregationalist church which upheld a strict doctrine of predestination that unsettled young Mary.

"The doctrine of unconditional election or predestination, greatly troubled me: for I was unwilling to be saved, if my brothers and sisters were to be numbered among those who were doomed to perpetual banishment from God" (Mary Baker Eddy, *Retrospection and Introspection*, p. 14). Her life later became characterized by the rejection of doctrines that are central to the Christian faith.

Christian Science Discovered

In 1866, while still married to Daniel Patterson, she discovered the principle of Christian Science after a serious fall allegedly brought her near death. Her account of the severity of the injuries was contradicted by the attending physician. Nevertheless, the principles "discovered" during this time were to be the basis of Christian Science. In 1875, her work *Science and Health* was published with the additional *Key to the Scriptures* added in 1883. For this work she claimed divine revelation.

"I should blush to write of *Science and Health with Key to the Scriptures* as I have, were it of human origin and I apart from God its author, but as I was only a scribe echoing the harmonies of Heaven in divine metaphysics, I cannot be super-modest of the Christian Science Textbook" (*Christian Science Journal*, Jan. 1901).

In 1879 in Charlestown, Massachusetts, the Church of Christ Scientist was organized and was then changed in 1892 to the First Church of Christ Scientist. The Church Manual was published in 1895 establishing the procedures of governing the church.

The Death of Mrs. Eddy

Although she taught that death is "an illusion, the life of life" (*Science and Health*, 584:9), Mrs. Eddy passed away December 3, 1910. Today there is a self-perpetuating board of directors which governs the church. There is no way to get an accurate number of Christian Scientists today since the Church Manual says, "Christian Scientists shall not report for publication the number of the members of the Mother Church, nor that of the branch churches" (Article VIII, Sect. 28-1911 ed.). Observers estimate worldwide membership at more than three million.

The Claims of Christian Science

Christian Science, like many other cults, claims further revelation that goes "beyond the Bible"—that is to say, new divine truth previously unrevealed.

On page 107, in her work *Science and Health*, Mrs. Eddy quotes the Apostle Paul:

"But I certify you, brethren, that the Gospel which was preached of me is not after man. For I neither received it of man, neither was I taught it, but by the revelation of Jesus Christ."

She follows the quotation with this claim:

"In the year 1866, I discovered the Christ Science or divine laws of Life, Truth, and Love and named my discovery Christian Science. God has been graciously preparing me during many years for the reception of this final revelation of the absolute divine Principle of scientific mental healing" (*Science and Health*, 107:1-6).

She goes on, "Whence came to me this heavenly conviction...When apparently near the confines of mortal existence, standing already within the shadow of the death-valley, I learned these truths in divine Science" (*Science and Health*, 108:1, 19-21).

She concludes:

"I won my way to absolute conclusions through divine revelation, reason, and demonstration. The Revelation of Truth in the understanding came to me gradually and apparently through Divine Power" (*Science and Health*, 109:20-23).

Mrs. Eddy's claims are clear: The revelation she received while near death was divine. She also claims exclusive truth: "Is there more than one school of Christian Science?...There can, therefore, be but one method in its teaching" (*Science and Health*, 112:3-5). Needless to say the one method is her method.

The Christian Science Church Manual states their purpose as "to commemorate the word and works of our master, which should reinstate primitive Christianity and its lost element of healing" (*The Christian Science Church Manual*, 89th ed., p. 17).

The following paragraph reveals Mrs. Eddy's monumental claims.

"Late in the nineteenth century I demonstrated the divine rules of Christian Science. They were submitted to the broadest practical test, and everywhere, when honestly applied under circumstances where demonstration was humanly possible, this science showed that truth had lost none of its divine and healing efficacy, even though centuries had passed away since Jesus practiced these rules on the hills of Judaea and in the valleys of Galilee" (*Science and Health*, 147:6-13).

Therefore, Christian Science claims to have restored the lost element in Christianity, namely healing, that when applied, demonstrates itself to work. Moreover, this knowledge of divine healing claims to have been revealed to Mrs. Eddy who is sharing this "exclusive truth" with the world. Thus, Christian Science claims to go further than the orthodox churches by reinstating that which was missing.

Source of Authority

Mrs. Eddy claimed that she derived her teachings from the Bible, which she considered her final authority. However, in practice, and as we have just seen above, she also claimed that her revelations were better and "higher" than the Bible. Where the Bible contradicted her beliefs, she felt free to dismiss its authority.

"The Bible has been my only authority. I have no other guide in 'The straight and narrow way' of Truth" (*Science and Health*, 126:28-31).

Although she claimed that the Bible was her guide, her view of Scripture was something less than desirable: "The material record of the Bible,...is no more important to our well-being than the history of Europe and America" (Mary Baker Eddy, *Miscellaneous Writings*, 1833-1896, p. 170:19-21).

"The decisions by vote of Church Councils as to what should and should not be considered Holy Writ; the manifest mistakes in the ancient versions; the thirty thousand different readings in the Old Testament, and the three hundred thousand in the New, — these facts show how a mortal and material sense stole into the divine record, with its own hue darkening to some extent the inspired pages" (*Science and Health*, 139:15-22).

Mrs. Eddy also assumes there are two different contradictory creation accounts in Genesis, "The Science of the first record proves the falsity of the second. If one is true, the other is false, for they are antagonistic" (*Science and Health*, 522:3-5). (For a thorough refutation of the so-called two-creation account theory, see our *Answers to Tough Questions*, pp. 170-196.)

In actuality, she does not obtain her teachings from the Bible even though the claim is made that "as adherents of Truth, we take the inspired Word of the Bible as our sufficient guide to eternal life" (*Science and Health*, 497: 3-4).

The fact is, the teachings of Christian Science are in direct contradiction to the Bible. The real authority in Christian Science is not the Bible, but the writings of Mrs. Eddy. She has this to say about her own work, *Science and Health*:

"...It is the voice of Truth to this age" (*Science and Health*, 456:27, 28).

"...The revealed Truth uncontaminated by human hypothesis" (*Science and Health*, 457:1-2).

"No human pen nor tongue taught me the Science contained in this book, SCIENCE AND HEALTH; and neither tongue nor pen can overthrow it" (*Science and Health*, 110: 16-19).

Christian Science does what so many of the cults do; it has a second authority which supersedes the Bible as the final authority in solving doctrinal matters. The writings of Mrs. Eddy constitute the final word as far as Christian Scientists are concerned, with the Bible relegated to a secondary status, although she paid lip service homage to the Bible.

Phineas Quimby

In a sermon delivered in June of 1890, Mrs. Eddy again made the claim to divine revelation: "Christian Science is irrevocable—unpierced by bold conjecture's sharp point, by bald philosophy, or by man's inventions. It is divinely true, and every hour in time and in eternity will witness more steadfastly to its practical truth" (Mary Baker Eddy, *Seven Messages to the Mother Church*, pp. 20-21). There is strong evidence to the contrary; that Mrs. Eddy's "divine revelation" is not original to her, but is a plagiarism of Phineas Quimby's writings and ideas.

Phineas Quimby was a self-professed healer who applied hypnosis and the power of suggestion in affecting his cures. He called his word, "The science of the Christ" and "Christian Science." Mrs. Eddy became an enthusiastic follower of Quimby in 1862 after her back injury was healed by him. She wrote letters to the Portland (Maine) Evening Courier praising Quimby and comparing him to Jesus Christ.

Upon his death she eulogized Quimby in a poem, titling it, "Lines on the Death of Dr. P. P. Quimby, who healed with the truth that Christ taught in contradistinction to all Isms." Eventually she attempted to separate any connection between herself and Quimby when charges of borrowing his ideas surfaced. However, the facts are otherwise.

In 1921, Horatio Dresser published *The Quimby Manuscripts*, which when compared with Mrs. Eddy's writings, revealed many parallels leading some to comment, "...as far as thought is concerned, *Science and Health* is practically all Quimby" (Ernest Sutherland Bates and John V. Dittermore, *Mary Baker Eddy: The Truth and The Tradition*, 1932, p. 156).

(For a thorough documentation of the Borrowing of Quimby's ideas we recommend Georgine Milmine, 1971, *The Life of Mary Baker G. Eddy*, Grand Rapids: Baker Book House reprint of a 1909 work, pp. 56-104).

Mrs. Eddy received the principles of Christian Science from some place other than the God of the Bible. Since her teachings contradict the teachings of God as revealed in the Bible, they are thereby condemned by the Bible and she is therefore a false teacher.

The Theology of Christian Science

Even though Christian Science claims to be a restatement of primitive, pure Christianity, it denies everything that is considered sacred to God's Word.

God

Mrs. Eddy defined God as, "The great I Am; the all-knowing, all-seeing, all acting, all-wise, all-loving, and eternal; Principle; Mind; Soul: Spirit (*Science and Health*, 587:5-8).

Elsewhere she calls God "Divine Principle, Life, Truth, Love, Soul, Spirit, Mind" (ibid., 115:13-14).

Mrs. Eddy claimed that the God she revealed through Christian Science was not pantheistic. (Pantheism is the belief that God is all of existent reality, including the material world. Hinduism, because it identifies God with the creation, is pantheistic.) In denying a pantheistic God Mrs. Eddy said:

At this period of enlightenment, a declaration from the pulpit that Christian Science is Pantheism is anomalous to those who know whereof they speak—who know that Christian Science is science, and therefore, is neither hypothetical nor dogmatical, but demonstrable, and looms above the mists of Pantheism higher than Ararat above the deluge (*Seven*

Messages to the Mother Church, Mary Baker Eddy, 1907, p. 10).

However, when Mrs. Eddy described her God, she clearly identified him with the creation. Her God actually is pantheistic. She said, "God is a divine Whole, and All, an all-pervading intelligence and love, a divine, infinite principle" (Mary Baker Eddy, *Miscellaneous Writings*, p. 16:21, 22).

The God of the Bible, on the other hand is infinite (Psalm 139:7-16), yet personal (Isaiah 45:20-25). He is the Creator, but He is not the creation (Isaiah 44:24). The God of the Bible and the God of Christian Science are not the same. The Apostle Paul declared the true God:

> The God who made the world and all things in it, since He is Lord of heaven and earth, does not dwell in temples made with hands; neither is He served by human hands, as though He needed anything, since He Himself gives to all life and breath and all things...(Acts 17:24, 25).

Jesus Christ

The Christian Science view of the person of Christ is wholly unbiblical: "Christ is the ideal truth that comes to heal sickness and sin through Christian Science, and attributes all power to God. Jesus is the name of the man who, more than all other men, has presented Christ, the true idea of God...Jesus is the human man, and Christ is the divine idea; hence the duality of Jesus the Christ" (*Science and Health*, 473:9-16).

Mrs. Eddy attempts to make a distinction between "Jesus" and "the Christ" as if they were two separate entities. This distinction is not possible for Jesus Christ is one person. Jesus is His name meaning "Yahweh is Salvation," Christ, His title, meaning "The Anointed One." The attempted distinction that Christian Scientists make between the two shows a complete lack of understanding of the Scriptures, such as Luke 2:11, 1 John 2:22, and 1 John 5:1.

Since Jesus and Christ are two different entities in Christian Science, the doctrine that Jesus Christ is God is rejected, "...the Christian believes that Christ is God...Jesus Christ is not God..." (*Science and Health*, 361:1, 2, 12).

In direct contradiction to the above statement, the Bible clearly teaches the docrine of the Holy Trinity. We do not believe in polytheism, or more than one God. We believe that in the nature of the one true God (Isaiah 43:10), there exists three eternal and distinct persons (Luke 3:22): the Father (2 Peter 1:17); the Word or Son (John 1:1, 14); and the Holy Spirit (Acts 5:3, 4). These three persons are the one God (Matthew 28:19).

Salvation

Concerning salvation, Mrs. Eddy said: "Life, Truth, and Love understood and demonstrated as supreme over all; sin, sickness and death destroyed" (*Science and Health*, p. 593:20-22). Since to the Christian Scientist there is no such thing as sin, salvation in the biblical sense is totally unnecessary. The teachings concerning salvation in Mrs. Eddy's writings are both ambiguous and inconsistent. She stated over and over again that sin is just an illusion (*Miscellaneous Writings*, 27:11-12, *Science and Health*, 71:2, 287:22, 23, 480:23, 24, etc.).

On the other hand, she states as quoted above, that salvation is "...sin, sickness and death destroyed." If sin is only an illusion, having no real existence, how can it be destroyed? Putting it another way, do you destroy something that does not exist? Since there is no harmonious teaching in Christian Science concerning salvation, it is difficult to evaluate it objectively. Nevertheless, the Christian Science view is a far cry from the Bible that teaches the reality of sin (Romans 3:23) and the need for a Savior (Acts 4:12).

Evil

In Christian Science there eixsts no evil: "Here also is found the path of the basal statement, the cardinal point in Christian Science, that matter and evil (including all inharmony, sin, disease, death) are unreal" (*Miscellaneous Writings*, p. 27). According to Christian Science, "Christ came to destroy the belief of sin" (*Science and Health*, p. 473). It is further emphasized "...evil is but an illusion, and it has no real basis. Evil is a false belief, God is not its author" (*Science and Health*, 480:23, 24).

Since evil is an illusion, the idea of the death of Christ on the cross for our sins is unnecessary:

> The material blood of Jesus was no more efficacious to cleanse from sin when it was shed upon "the accursed tree" than when it was flowing in his veins as he went daily about his Father's business (*Science and Health*, 25:6-8).

In distinction, the Bible teaches that evil is real (1 John 5:19) and that we would be without salvation if Jesus Christ had not died on the cross for our sins (Hebrews 9:22). As Christians we can rejoice in the good news that Jesus Christ "gave himself for our sins, that He might deliver us out of this present evil age, according to the will of our God and Father, to whom be the glory forevermore. Amen" (Galatians 1:4, 5).

Christian Science and Healing

"Our Master... practiced Christian healing... but left no definite rule for demonstrating this Principle of healing and preventing disease. This rule remained to be discovered by Christian Science" (*Science and Health*, 147:24-29).

In a section entitled "Fruitage" in *Science and Health* the following claim is made:

> "Thousands of letters could be presented in testimony of the healing efficacy of Christian Science and particularly concerning the vast number of people who have been reformed and healed through the perusal or study of this book" (*Science and Health*, p. 600).

Followed by this claim are approximately 100 pages of testimonials of healing of every conceivable disease by those who have embraced the principles of Christian Science. The obvious question arises: Can Christian Science heal? While many of the healings in Christian Science can be explained without appealing to the miraculous, there are some accounts of seemingly true healings.

If this be the case, then it would be an example of the "signs and false wonders" the Apostle Paul spoke about (2 Thessalonians 2:9). Satan is the great counterfeiter and his attempt to duplicate the works of God and the miracle of healing is no exception. We all want to be healthy, but not at the cost of abandoning Christ.

Conclusion

Christian Science is neither Christian nor scientific because every important doctrine of historic Christianity is rejected by Christian Science. The claim of divine revelation by Mrs. Eddy is contradicted by the facts that clearly attest she does not represent the God of the Bible. Although she speaks in the name of Jesus, her teachings conflict with His in every respect.

Fortunately, Jesus warned us ahead of time about people like Mrs. Eddy: "Beware of the false prophets, who come to you in sheep's clothing, but inwardly are ravenous wolves. You will know them by their fruits" (Matthew 7:15, 16 NASB).

Christian Science Terms

Animal Magnetism — According to Christian Science, animal magnetism, which is wrong thinking, causes an individual to experience the illusion of evil. Malicious animal magnetism can kill those it is practiced against.

At-one-ment — In Christian Science and other gnostic cults, it is the unity between the mind of God and the mind of man as demonstrated by Christ.

Christian Science Journal — Periodical of Christian Science, used for recruitment of new members.

Christian Science Monitor — Newspaper published by Christian Science, highly regarded in the secular world, with little religious propaganda.

Christian Science Sentinel — Periodical of Christian Science, used for recruitment of new members.

Eddy, Mary Baker — Founder of Christian Science. Mrs. Eddy (her third married name) said she discovered Christian Science as a result of a miraculous healing she supposedly received after a fall. She authored the text *Science and Health with Key to the Scriptures* that Christian Scientists revere above the Bible.

Immortal Mind — God in Christian Science theology.

Mortal Mind — According to Christian Science, it is the

source of the illusions of evil, sickness, sin and death.

Quimby, P. P. — Early 19th century mesmerist and psychic healer from whom Mary Baker Eddy learned the principles she later claimed were revealed from God as Christian Science.

Science and Health with Key to the Scriptures — Contains the teachings of Mary Baker Eddy, the founder of Christian Science. The book is regarded as a revelation with more authority than the Bible.

CHAPTER FIFTEEN

Unity

History

The Unity School of Christianity was founded by Charles and Myrtle Fillmore. Charles Sherlock Fillmore was born near St. Cloud, Minnesota in 1854. He married Mary Caroline Page (or "Myrtle") in 1881.

The early years of their marriage recorded many financial ups and downs until they finally established a modest real estate office in Kansas City, Missouri. Myrtle's family had a history of tuberculosis and she herself was eventually stricken ill with the dreaded disease. She also contracted malaria and was given, by her doctor, only six months to live.

In 1886, the Fillmores went to a lecture which was to change their lives dramatically. The speaker, E. B. Weeks, said to the crowd that night, "I am a child of God and therefore I do not inherit sickness." Myrtle believed the statement and continued to recite it over and over again. Eventually she was healed.

At first, Charles refused to accept his wife's new technique but he was willing to investigate it, along with other religions. After an extensive study of the science of mind and Eastern religions, including Hinduism and Buddhism, he decided to try his wife's meditation technique. After continued meditation, his withered leg was healed, and he joined Myrtle in founding a new religious system, later called the Unity School of Christianity.

Borrowing heavily from Christian Science and New Thought, (a 19th century metaphysical healing movement developed from the system of mental healer Phineas Quimby), the Fillmores added their own interpretations, including the Eastern concept of reincarnation, and presented their teachings first to the people of Missouri and then to the world. Under pressure from Christian Science founder, Mary Baker Eddy, the Fillmores stopped using terms common to Christian Science.

They did enjoy a long relationship with the New Thought movement, but eventually chose independent status as a religious movement not affiliated with any other religion. The movement went through several names; Modern Thought (1889), Christian Science Thought (1890), and Thought (1891), and eventually took the name Unity in 1895.

Myrtle Fillmore died in 1931 whereupon Charles married Cora Dedrick, his private secretary. Charles Fillmore died in 1948. The leadership of Unity was taken over by the Fillmores' two sons, Lowell and Rickert, and subsequently experienced a rapid growth. Today, Unity has some two million adherents worldwide, with its headquarters at Unity Village, in Lee's Summit, Missouri, a suburb of Kansas City.

The Beliefs of Unity

Unity claims that beliefs and belief systems are not important. What matters is that the Unity system works, even if the practitioner doesn't believe everything Charles and Myrtle Fillmore taught. However, in actual practice Unity is a strict religious system with clear-cut beliefs to which all long-term members eventually subscribe.

It was 30 years before Charles Fillmore drew up a statement of faith which was qualified with the following: "We are hereby giving warning that we shall not be bound to this tentative statement of what Unity believes. We may change our mind tomorrow on some of the points, and if we do, we shall feel free to make a new statement" (James Dillet Freeman, *What Is Unity?*, Lee's Summit, Missouri, n.d., p. 5).

Contrary to Fillmore's statement is the Bible's continued assertion that what a person believes is important.

"He who believes in the Son has eternal life; but he who does not obey the Son shall not see life; but the wrath of God abides on him" (John 3:36 NASB. See also Hebrews 11:6. [For further documentation on why right belief is vital to the Christian faith, see our work, *Answers to Tough Questions*, pp. 149-151]).

The basic world view of Unity is that of gnosticism. Gnosticism is a theological term referring to a system of belief that qualitatively separates the spirit from the material. It also believes knowledge is secret and only obtainable by a select few. Gnostics generally believe that what is spiritual is good and what is material is bad. Christian Science, another gnostic cult, goes so far as to say that the material world doesn't even exist!

According to gnosticism, God is impersonal and one's eventual goal is to reach oneness with this impersonal God. Gnostics view Jesus Christ as a human being who possessed, in some great way, the expression or presence of God. To them, Jesus refers to the man and Christ refers to the divine influence. Rather than agreeing with the Bible by declaring that Jesus is the Christ (1 John 5:1), gnostics, including Unity, separate Jesus from the Christ.

Unity is not as interested in theology as it is in prosperity and happiness. A survey of the literature of Unity will clearly show that the stress is on material and worldly happiness, not spiritual happiness.

The Bible

"We believe that the Word of God is the thought of God expressed in creative ideas and that these ideas are the primal attributes of all enduring entities in the universe, visible and invisible. The Logos of the first chapter of the Gospel of John is the God idea of Christ that produced Jesus, the perfect man. We believe the Scriptures are the testimonials of men who have in a measure apprehended the divine Logos but that their writings should not be taken as final" (Unity's *Statement of Faith*, part 27).

The Scriptures testify to the fact that it is God who is their ultimate author, "All Scripture is given by inspiration of God" (2 Timothy 3:16), "...When you received from us the Word of Men, but for what it really is, the Word of God (1 Thessalonians 2:13 NASB).

God

The doctrine of God in Unity is similar to that of Christian Science and other gnostic cults. Rather than believing in the Bible's infinite and personal creator, Unity adheres to the belief that God is impersonal.

This can be readily seen by a statement from Myrtle Fillmore. "Though personal to each one of us, God is it, neither male nor female, but principle" (Myrtle Fillmore, *How to Let God Help You*, 1956, p. 25). The *Metaphysical Dictionary*, a work of Charles Fillmore states, "The Father is Principle, the Son is that Principle revealed in creative plan, the Holy Spirit is the executive power of both Father and Son carrying out the creative plan" (*Metaphysical Bible Dictionary*, p. 629). One Unity publication states, "God is all and all is God" (*Unity*, August, 1974, p. 40).

Fillmore also said, "God is not loving...God does not love anybody or anything. God is the love in everybody and everything. God is love...God exercises none of His attributes except through the inner consciousnes of the universe and man" (*Jesus Christ Heals*, Unity School of Christianity, 1944, pp. 31,32).

The Fillmores and other Unity writers confuse the attributes of God with God Himself. God is more than attributes such as love. He is personal (Exodus 3:14). He is not to be equated with the impersonal "everything" for He has a separate existence apart from creation (Isaiah 44: 1-28; Romans 1:18-25). Unity would deny Him His rightful position as creator, sustainer, and Lord of the universe.

Jesus Christ

"The Bible says that God so loved the world that He gave His only begotten Son, but the Bible does not here refer to Jesus of Nazareth, the outer man; it refers to the Christ, the spiritual identity of Jesus, whom he acknowledged in all his ways, and brought forth into his outer self, until even the flesh of his body was lifted up, purified, spiritualized, and redeemed, thus he became Jesus Christ, the word made flesh.

"And we are to follow into this perfect state and become like Him, for in each of us is the Christ, the only begotten Son. We can, through Jesus Christ, our Redeemer and example, bring forth the Christ within us, the true self of all is perfect, as Jesus Christ commanded his followers to be" (*Unity*, Vol. 57, no. 5, 464, and Vol. 72, no. 2, p. 8).

The Bible states however, "Who is the liar, but the one who denies that Jesus is the Christ..." (1 John 2:22). Jesus was called the Christ from the time of his birth (Luke 2:11, 26). The only way one can be born of God is to believe that Jesus is the Christ (1 John 5:1).

Unity teaches that within all of us there is an "inner Christ," equated with perfection, a divine awareness (Elizabeth Sand Turner, *What Unity Teaches*, Lee's Summit, Missouri, n.d., p. 9). All of us are capable of attaining that "inner Christ," that divine awareness and perfection.

The New Testament maintains that Jesus is different from us by the fact that He is God by His very nature: "In the beginning was the Word, and the Word was with God, and the Word was God" (John 1:1). Jesus Christ is the unique Son of God (John 1:14). No one else can be the Son of God as Jesus Christ is the Son of God (John 5:18-23). He alone is the "image of the invisible God" (Colossians 1:15), the "radiance of His glory and the exact representation of His nature" (Hebrews 1:3).

Salvation

In Unity, salvation is unnecessary: "There is no sin, sickness or death" (*Unity*, Vol. 47, No. 5, p. 403). There is no need for the death of Christ on the cross to take away sin. Unity said of the atonement of Christ, "The atonement is the union of man with God the Father, in Christ. Stating it in terms of mind, we should say that the Atonement is the At-one-ment or agreement of reconciliation of man's mind with Divine Mind through the superconsciousness of Christ's mind" (*What Practical Christianity Stands For*, p. 5).

Here again we have Unity in direct contradiction to the Bible that acknowledges sin as a reality, "For *all* have sinned and come short of the glory of God" (Romans 3:23). Furthermore, "The wages of sin is death, but the gift of God is eternal life through Jesus Christ our Lord" (Romans 6:23). If a person does not come to Christ for salvation he will be lost in his sin, "For unless you believe that I am He, you shall die in your sins" (John 8:24 NASB).

Reincarnation

Unity's statement of faith shows that they believe salvation involves reincarnation. "We believe that the dissolution of spirit, soul, and body caused by death, is annulled by rebirth of the same spirit and soul in another body here on earth. We believe the repeated incarnations of man to be a merciful provision of our loving Father to the end that all may have opportunity to attain immortality through regeneration, as did Jesus. This corruptible must put on incorruption" (*Unity's Statement of Faith*, Article 22).

Reincarnation teaches that only through many lifetimes can one rid himself of the debt for all of his sins. However, the Bible teaches that through Jesus Christ we can be rid of all of our sins at one time (1 John 1:8-10). His purpose for dying on the cross was as a sacrifice for our sins (Acts 3:18, 19).

Jesus Christ is the only Savior we ever need because "He abides forever, holds His priesthood permanently. Hence, also, He is able to save forever those who draw near to God through Him, since He always lives to make intercession for them" (Hebrews 7:24, 25). We have the promise of God Himself that our salvation has been guaranteed through faith in the sacrifice of Jesus Christ on the cross (1 Peter 1:2-6).

Prosperity

Another major tenet of Unity is that no one need be poor. Charles Fillmore, in his book *Prosperity*, perverted the 23rd Psalm in expressing this belief.

"The Lord is my banker, my credit is good.
He maketh me to lie down in the consciousness of omnipresent abundance;
He giveth me the key to His strongbox.
He restoreth my faith in His riches;
He guideth me in the paths of prosperity for His name's sake.
Yea though I walk in the very shadow of debt,
I shall fear no evil, for Thou art with me:
Thy silver and Thy Gold, they secure me.

Thou preparest a way for me in the presence of the collector;
Thou fillest my wallet with plenty; my measure runneth over.
Surely goodness and plenty will follow me all the days of my life;
And I shall do business in the name of the Lord forever."

The message of the Bible concerns our spiritual prosperity, not our material prosperity. As Christians, our desires are to be transformed spiritually by faith in Jesus Christ and the working of the Holy Spirit in our lives. The greed and self-centeredness exhibited by Fillmore's poem is in direct contradiction to the humility and God-centeredness the Bible teaches. If one's central desire is to serve the Lord and to express His love to others, one's material needs diminish and material prosperity doesn't even matter. The Apostle Paul put it like this:

Not that I speak from want; for I have learned to be content in whatever circumstances I am. I know how to get along with humble means, and I also know how to live in prosperity; in any and every circumstance I have learned the secret of being filled and going hungry, both of having abundance and suffering need. I can do all things through Him who Strengthens me...And my God shall supply all your needs according to His riches in glory in Christ Jesus (Philippians 4:11-13,19 NAS).

Conclusion

The Unity School of Christianity has no right to use the name Christian to describe its organization, for it is decidedly not Christian. Unfortunately, many Christians read the publications of Unity without realizing it is a non-Christian cult denying the basic beliefs of Christianity.

In the first publication that proceeded from the Fillmores, the non-Christian basis was revealed when they said, "We see the good in all religions and we want everyone to feel free to find the Truth for himself wherever he may be led to find it" (*Modern Thought*, 1889, p. 42). In contrast to this, Jesus of Nazareth said, "I am the Way, and the Truth, and the Life; no one comes to the Father, but through me" (John 14:6 NASB).

It is clear that Unity and Christianity are opposed to each other on the basic issues with no possible way of reconciling Unity as being part of Christianity.

Cult Ministry Referrals

Acts 17, P.O. Box 2183, La Mesa, California 92041.
(Emphasis: General cults and general occult)

Anderson, Einar, 1124-H North Louise Street, Glendale, California 91207.
(Emphasis: Mormonism)

C.A.I., P.O. Box 3295, Chico, California 95927.
(Emphasis: Jehovah's Witnesses and Mormonism)

Ron Carlson, C.M.I., 7601 Superior Terrace, Even Prairie, Minnesota 55344.
(Emphasis: General cult and general occult)

Robert Passantino, C.A.R.I.S., P.O. Box 2067, Costa Mesa, California 92626.
(Emphasis: General cult, general occult, apologetics, and theology)

Jim Valentine, C.A.R.I.S., P.O. Box 1659, Milwaukee, Wisconsin 53201.
(Emphasis: General cult, general occult, and Eastern philosophy)

Bill Cetnar, Route 2 Wierlake, Kunkletown, Pennsylvania 18058.
(Emphasis: Jehovah's Witnesses)

Christian Information Network, P.O. Box 421, Pine Lake, Georgia 30072.
(Emphasis: General cult and general occult)

Walter Martin, Christian Research Institute, P.O. Box 500, San Juan Capistrano, California 92693.
(Emphasis: General cult and general occult)

James Bjornstad, Institute for Contemporary Christianity, P.O. Box A, Oakland, New Jersey 07436.
(Emphasis: General cult, general occult, and philosophy)

Marvin Cowan, P.O. Box 21052, Salt Lake City, Utah 84121.
(Emphasis: Mormonism)

Bob Witt, Ex-Mormons for Jesus, P.O. Box 10177, Clearwater, Florida 33519.
(Emphasis: Mormonism)

Ed Decker, Saints Alive, P.O. Box 113, Issaquah, Washington 98027.
(Emphasis: General cult and Mormonism)

Wally Tope, Front Line, P.O. Box 1100, La Canada Flintridge, California 91011.
(Emphasis: Jehovah's Witnesses, Mormonism, and Christian Science)

Edmond Gruss, Los Angeles Baptist College, P.O. Box 878, Newhall, California 91321.
(Emphasis: General cult and general occult specializing in Jehovah's Witnesses)

Homer Duncan, Missionary Crusader, 4606 Ave. H, Lubbock, Texas 79404.
(Emphasis: Jehovah's Witnesses)

Jerald Tanner, Modern Microfilm Company, P.O. Box 1884, Salt Lake City, Utah 84110.
(Emphasis: Mormonism)

J. L. Williams, New Directions Evangelistic Association, P.O. Box 2347, Burlington, North Carolina 27215.
(Emphasis: General cult and general occult specializing in The Way International).

Kurt Van Gorden, PACE, 1944 North Tustin Ave., Suite 118, Orange, California 92665.
(Emphasis: General cult and general occult specializing in The Way International and The Unification Church)

Personal Freedom Outreach, P.O. Box 26062, St. Louis, Missouri 63136.

(Emphasis: Jehovah's Witnesses and Mormonism)

Brooks Alexander, Spiritual Counterfeits Project, P.O. Box 4308, Berkeley, California 94704.
(Emphasis: General cult, general occult, sociology, and Eastern thought)

Arthur Budvarson, Utah Christian Tract Society, P.O. Box 725, La Mesa, California 92041.
(Emphasis: Mormonism)

Duane Magnani, Witness Incorporated, P.O. Box 597, Clayton, California 94517.
(Emphasis: Jehovah's Witnesses)

Annotated
Cults Bibliography

Adair, James R. and Ted Miller, ed. *We Found Our Way Out*
(Grand Rapids, Michigan: Baker Book House, 1964).

These are testimonies of people who were into cults and
have come to a saving knowledge of Jesus Christ. It covers
Mormonism, Jehovah's Witnesses, Christian Science,
Humanism, Communism, Seventh-day Adventism,
Modernism, Armstrongism, Satanism, Agnosticism,
Theosophism, and Hippies.

Anderson, Einar. *The Inside Story of Mormonism* (Grand
Rapids, Michigan: Kregel Publications, 1973).

This is an excellent story of a man who was a Mormon,
why he got into Mormonism, what the Mormons believe,
why he left it, and why he knows it is not Christian. It
discusses the history of Mormonism, Mormon beginnings,
Mormon Articles of Faith, and false Bible interpretations by
the Mormons.

Benwar, Paul. *Ambassadors of Armstrongism* (Nutley, New
Jersey: Presbyterian and Reformed Publishing Company,
1975).

A good treatment of the history and teachings of the
Worldwide Church of God. Includes doctrine of Scripture,
God, Holy Spirit, Christ, angels, man, sin, salvation, the
church, future things, special teachings and refutes all the
major doctrinal errors of the Worldwide Church of God.

Bjornstad, James. *Counterfeits at Your Door* (Ventura, California: Gospel Light Publications, 1979).

This is an excellent treatment by one of the leading authorities in cult apologetics. It discusses Jehovah's Witnesses and Mormonism. It tells basically what they believe on the major doctrines of Christianity and why they are not biblical, and how to answer them.

_____ *The Moon is Not the Son: A Close Look at the Teachings of Rev. Sun Myung Moon and the Unification Church* (Minneapolis, Minnesota: Bethany Fellowship Incorporated, 1976).

Excellent treatment of Moon's complicated theology, history and practices of the Church and good Christian responses.

Boa, Kenneth. *Cults, World Religions and You* (Wheaton, Illinois: Victor Books, a Division of Scripture Press Publications, 1977).

This book covers non-Christian religions of the east, pseudo-Christian religions of the west, the major cults— Mormonism, Jehovah's Witnesses, etc. occult religion and systems, and new religions and cults like TM, Hare Krishna, as seen from a conservative Christian point of view.

Cowan, Marvin. *Mormon Claims Answered* (Salt Lake City, Utah: Marvin Cowan Publisher, 1975).

This is a very good technical treatment of the beliefs of Mormonism. It goes into origin and history, doctrine of God, the Bible, the Book of Mormon, the church and salvation. With excellent Christian answers that show step-by-step how to witness to a Mormon who is knowledgeable.

Cowdrey, Davis, and Scales with Gretchen Passantino. *Who Really Wrote the Book of Mormon?* (Santa Ana, California: Vision House Publishers, 1977 and 1980).

This is an excellent book on the origins of the Book of Mormon. It deals briefly with Mormon history and extensively with the Book of Mormon demonstrating it is not a revelation from God. The theory also says it was not written or translated by Joseph Smith, the founder of Mormonism, but instead was plagiarized by Smith and his colleagues and stolen from a novelist named Solomon Spaulding. This is the best book on this particular theory and has great evidence to support it.

Dencher, Ted. *Why I Left Jehovah's Witnesses* (Fort Washington, Pennsylvania: Christian Literature Crusade, 1966).

Testimony of a man who was in Jehovah's Witnesses and why he left. Presents the major teachings and history of the Jehovah's Witnesses and why they are not Christian. This is an excellent book to use as a study resource for a Christian. It should not be given to a Jehovah's Witness because the author's tone of voice is sometimes sarcastic.

Duddy, Neil and the Spiritual Counterfeits Project. *The God-Men: an Inquiry Into Witness Lee and the Local Church* (Downers Grove, Illinois: InterVarsity Press, 1981).

This is the most thorough treatment of Witness Lee's teachings and the Local Church. There is concern as to whether this group should be classified as a non-Christian cult or not. Duddy examines the different sides of that position in his book. It deals with the Local Church doctrine, history of the movement, and evaluation of its teaching.

Edwards, Christopher. *Crazy for God: the Nightmare of Cult Life* (Inglewood, New Jersey: Prentice Hall Incorporated, 1979).

This is a story of a young man who joined the Unification Church, why he joined it, what happened to him while he was in it and how he got out of it. In the very last chapter he says he does have religious faith now, but does not go into detail.

Enroth, Ronald. *The Lure of the Cults* (Chappaqua, New York: Christian Herald Books, 1979).

Dr. Enroth is a sociologist teaching at Westmont College, department of Sociology. An excellent source for materials on the sociological aspects of the cults from the Christian perspective. This book is organized by topic, not according to cults, and he mentions many cults throughout the book. It discusses why people get involved with the cults and how one can try to teach someone who is in a cult.

_____ *Youth, Brainwashing, and the Extremist Cults* (Grand Rapids, Michigan: Zondervan Publishing House, 1977).

This book discusses case histories from Hare Krishna, Children of God, The Alamo Foundation, The Unification Church, The Way International, and The Divine Light Mission, and then talks about the sociological factors influencing the growth and rise of the cults, again, from a conservative evangelical Christian point of view.

Fraser, Gordon. *Is Mormonism Christian?* (Chicago, Illinois: Moody Press, 1957 and 1977).

This is a good general treatment from an evangelical Christian position. It does not contain a great deal of detail on doctrinal teachings, but it contains all the essentials. It's easy to read, does not have very many footnotes, and it's not very technical.

_____ *Sects of the Church of the Latter-Day Saints* (Eugene, Oregon: Industrial Litho Incorporated, 1978).

Discusses the reorganized Church of the Latter-Day Saints, and the Mormon polygamous sects. This is the best Christian treatment available on Mormonism. It is a very good book.

Gruss, Edmond. *Apostles of Denial* (Nutley, New Jersey: Presbyterian and Reformed, 1978).

This is the best single volume on Jehovah's Witnesses available today. Gruss used to be a Jehovah's Witness. He is a professor of apologetics at a Christian seminary. It is thorough and exhaustive and treats the history and all the doctrines, major and minor, in Jehovah's Witnesses from a Christian biblical perspective. It is an excellent book.

_____ *Cults and the Occults in the Age of Aquarius* (Nutley, New Jersey: Presbyterian and Reformed Publishing Company, 1974).

This is an excellent small paperback set up to be used as a study book for a Bible study. It covers Jehovah's Witnesses, Mormonism, Christian Science, the Unity Church, Herbert W. Armstrong and the Worldwide Church of God, Spiritualism, Seventh-day Adventism, Astrology, Baha'i, the occult, Scientology, and then gives a Christian response. Revised edition published in 1980.

_____ *The Jehovah's Witnesses and Prophetic Speculation* (Nutley, New Jersey: Presbyterian and Reformed Publishing Company, 1972).

This deals specifically with the Jehovah's Witnesses continual false prophecies, especially about when the end of the world is coming. It is thoroughly documented and is a good additional resource on that subject.

_____ *We Left Jehovah's Witnesses: a Non-prophet Organization* (Nutley, New Jersey: Presbyterian and Reformed Publishing Company, 1974).

This contains testimonies of several people who were Jehovah's Witnesses and became Christians. In addition to giving testimonies, the testimonies contain good information on what Jehovah's Witnesses teach and how to reach someone who is a Jehovah's Witness.

Hefley, James C. *The Youthnappers* (Wheaton, Illinois: Victor Books, A Division of Scripture Press Publications, 1977).

From an evangelical point of view it gives a brief survey of some of the new cults: The Unification Church, Hare Krishna, Divine Light Mission, TM, Children of God, etc. This is definitely a quick overview survey. The author is a good writer and good at reviewing general movements; however, he is not an expert on the cults.

Hoekma, Anthony A. *Christian Science* (Grand Rapids, Michigan: William B. Eerdmans Publishing Company, 1963).

This is a condensation and slight revision of the section of Christian Science from his standard work, the *Four Major Cults.*

_____ *Jehovah's Witnesses* (Grand Rapids, Michigan: William B. Eerdmans Publishing Company, 1963).

This is a reprint and a slight revision of his chapter on Jehovah's Witnesses in his book the *Four Major Cults.*

_____ *Mormonism* (Grand Rapids, Michigan: William B. Eerdmans Publishing Company, 1963).

This is excerpted and revised from his classic hardcover book, the *Four Major Cults.*

_____ *The Four Major Cults* (Grand Rapids, Michigan: William B. Eerdmans Publishing Company, 1963).

This is one of the classic old-time books on the cults. It discusses Mormonism, Seventh-day Adventism, Christian Science, Jehovah's Witnesses and the distinctive traits of the cults and approaching the cultist. This is done from a conservative Christian point of view.

Hopkins, Joseph. *The Armstrong Empire: A Look at the Worldwide Church of God* (Grand Rapids, Michigan: William B. Eerdmans Publishing Company, 1974).

It has extensive history on the Worldwide Church of God and Herbert W. Armstrong. It deals extensively with British Israelism, a doctrine that says the Jews are now the Europeans. It refutes the basic Armstrong doctrines of God, Christ, the Holy Spirit, Satan, salvation and Scripture.

Hunt, Dave. *The Cult Explosion* (Eugene, Oregon: Harvest House Publishers, 1980).

This treats the spiritual aspects of the cult movements, rather than dealing systematically and theologically with specific cults. This is a good overview of the spiritual battle going on for the lives of those who are caught up in the cults. This book also has a study guide, available from the same publisher, to go with it so it can be used in classes.

Lewis, Gordon R. *Confronting the Cults* (Grand Rapids, Michigan: Baker Book House, 1966).

This is another classic dealing with major cults — Jehovah's Witnesses, Mormonism, Christian Science, Seventh-day Adventism, Unity and Spiritualism. It deals with the cults from an evangelical point of view and discusses the major doctrines of each of the cults and the Christian responses to them.

_____ *What Everyone Should Know About Transcendental Meditation* (Ventura, California: Gospel Light Publications, 1975).

Excellent Christian treatment of TM by an excellent Christian scholar. He is not necessarily an expert on TM but has documented facts and good documentation.

Martin, Walter. *The Kingdom of the Cults* (Grand Rapids,

Michigan: Bethany Fellowship Incorporated, 1965. Revised edition 1975).

This is the classic standard text on the major non-Christian cults from an evangelical point of view. It discusses Jehovah's Witnesses, Christian Science, Mormonism, Spiritism, Father Divine, Theosophy, Buddhism, Swedenborgianism, Baha'i, Black Muslims, Unity School of Christianity, Worldwide Church of God, Seventh-day Adventism, Unitarianism, and Rosicrucians. Everybody who wants to learn about the cults should read this book.

_____ The New Cults (Santa Ana, California: Vision House Publishers Incorporated, 1980).

This book is probably the most comprehensive evangelical or theological treatment of the new cults. It treats The Way International, Hare Krishna, TM, EST, Children of God, Silva Mind Control, Ascended Masters (I AM), Roy Masters, Church of the Living Word, Nicheren Shoshu Buddhism, Reincarnation, and the Local Church. This book documents the main beliefs of all these groups on the central doctrines of the Christian faith and the biblical responses to them.

_____ The Rise of the Cults (Santa Ana, California: Vision House Publishers Incorporated, 1980).

This is a condensation and revision of some of the same topics covered in the Kingdom of the Cults. It discusses Jehovah's Witnesses, Worldwide Church of God, Christian Science, Mormonism, Unity, Spiritism, Baha'i. This is an excellent quick reference to document what these particular cults believe on all the major doctrines of the Christian faith and why they are not Christian.

Miller, Calvin. Transcendental Hesitation: A Biblical Appraisal of TM and Eastern Mysticism (Grand Rapids, Michigan: Zondervan Publishing House, 1977).

This is another good treatment of TM. It includes more history and documentation.

Miller, William McElwee. The Baha'i Faith: Its History and Teachings (Pasadena, California: William Carey Libarary, 1974).

This is a history of the Bah'i movement, done by a conservative evangelical Christian who was a missionary for 40 years in Iran. It is the most comprehensive treatment of Bah'ism available in English.

_____ *What is the Baha'i World Faith?* (Santa Ana, California: Christian Apologetics: Research and Information Service, 1977).

This is a short booklet explaining basically what Baha'ism teaches, why it is not Christian and how to witness to someone who is a Baha'i.

Milmine, Georgine. *The Life of Mary Baker G. Eddy and the History of Christian Science* (Grand Rapids, Michigan: Baker Book House, copyright 1909 by Doubleday, reprinted 1971 by Baker Books).

This is a classic, exhaustively documented history of the founder of Christian Science. It is done by a journalist from a non-Christian point of view. It points out all the historical inaccuracies and problems in the life of Mary Baker Eddy and Christian Science. This is an excellent historical resource.

Needleman, Jacob. *The New Religions* (New York, New York: E. P. Dutton and Company Inc., 1970).

This is a non-Christian book talking about the new eastern religions and cultic movements sweeping the U.S. It's divided topically and covers the major eastern religions such as: Hinduism, Buddhism, Sufism, as well as the occult, Zen Buddhism, TM, Meher Baba, Subud, and Krishnamurti.

Passantino, Robert and Gretchen. *Answers to the Cultist at Your Door* (Eugene, Oregon: Harvest House Publishers, 1981).

This book deals with Jehovah's Witnesses, Mormons, Hare Krishna, The Way International, and how to help your loved ones in a cult. This book is written on an easy-to-understand level. It contains testimonies of people who have left the cults. It tells specifically what the cults believe and why they are not Christian. It does not depend on the readers' knowing Greek, Hebrew, or extensive theology. It is an especially good book for a person who has not studied the cults much. It will also satisfy those with more extensive theological training.

Peterson, William J. *Those Curious New Cults* (New Canaan, Connecticut: Keats Publishers Incorporated, 1973 and 1975).

Includes why people were turned on by the new cults: Astrology, Edgar Cayce, Spiritualism, Witchcraft, Satanism, Scientology, Armstrongism, Children of God, Hare Krishna, Zen Buddhism, TM, Meher Baba, Baha'i, Gurdjieff the philosopher, The Divine Light Mission, and the Unification Church. This is a quick synopsis of some of the major features of all of these different cults. It is not in-depth. It does not deal with all of the areas of doctrinal deviation from the Bible, but it is a good Christian introduction.

Ridenour, Fritz. *So What's the Difference?* (Ventura, California: Gospel Light Publications, 1967).

This book deals with the most common cults and major religions of the world. It does treat Roman Catholicism as a cult. It is a small paperback that is easy to read.

Ropp, Harry L. *The Mormon Papers: Are the Mormon Scriptures Reliable?* (Downers Grove, Illinois: InterVarsity Press, 1977).

Another treatment of Mormon sacred writings, including the Book of Mormon, from an evangelical Christian point of view.

Rosten, Leo ed. *Religions in America* (New York, New York: Simon and Schuster, 1962-1963).

A non-Christian book. It covers 20 religious movements in the U.S., including Protestants, evangelicals, Catholics, and major cults. This is not an objective book. Each entry was submitted by a leader from that particular cult or religion.

Schnell, William. *Thirty Years a Watchtower Slave* (Grand Rapids, Michigan: Baker Book House, 1971).

This is the testimony of a man who was a Jehovah's Witness for 30 years, until he came to salvation in Jesus Christ. It tells why he was in it for so long, what held him in it, why he got out, and the freedom he then had in Jesus Christ.

Sire, James W. *Scripture Twisting: Twenty Ways the Cults Misread the Bible* (Downers Grove, Illinois: InterVarsity Press, 1980).

This is a specialized book. Written on a very simple level it discusses the way that cults try to use the Bible to support their beliefs and teachings.

Sparks, Jack. *The Mindbenders* (Nashville, Tennessee: Thomas Nelson Publishers, 1977 and 1979).

This is a standard current book on the new cults. It includes The Unification Church, The Way International, Children of God, The Local Church, TM, Divine Light Mission, Hare Krishna, People's Temple. Sparks deals with this from a sociological, psychological, and traditional church history point of view. He examines the cults' arguments theologically and gives biblical responses to them. He also points out how the Church throughout history has dealt with similar heresies.

Spittler, Russel P. *Cults and Isms: Twenty Alternatives to Evangelical Christianity* (Grand Rapids, Michigan: Baker Book House, 1962).

Discusses Mormonism, Seventh-day Adventism, Spiritualism, Christian Science, Jehovah's Witnesses, Unity, Moral Rearmament, Theosophy, Baha'i, Zen Buddhism, Anglo-Israelism, Astrology, Father Divine, Swedenborgianism, secular modernism, Humanism, Roman Catholicism, Unitarian Universalism, liberalism, and neo-orthodoxy. This book is one of the standard works. It's outdated, but does deal with cults still popular today. He examines things from a conservative Christian point of view.

Stoner, Carroll and Jo Anne Parke. *All God's Children* (Radnor, Pennsylvania: Chilton Book Company, 1977).

This book talks about the new religions, such as Unification Church and the Children of God. It discusses deprogramming, readjusting, and what to do if your child is in a cult. It discusses the upsurge in cults today. This is not a Christian book. It does contain valuable and useful information.

Tanner, Jerald and Sandra. *Mormonism — Shadow or Reality?* (Salt Lake City, Utah: Modern Microfilm Company, 1972).

This giant 600-page book contains all the documentation needed from Mormon sources on Mormon beliefs, history, and practices. It is an excellent treatise on all their historical major and minor doctrines, using primary Mormon sources for documentation. It is written from a Christian perspective but is not a theological or doctrinal book.

_____ *The Changing World of Mormonism* (Chicago, Illinois: Moody Press, 1980).

This is a condensation for laymen of the larger book, *Mormonism — Shadow or Reality?* It is still in-depth, extensive, and technical, but more readable than *Shadow or Reality.*

Thomas, F. W. *Masters of Deception: An Exposé of the Jehovah's Witnesses* (Grand Rapids, Michigan: Baker Book House).

This is a good treatment of the major and minor doctrines of the Jehovah's Witnesses from an evangelical Christian perspective. This book is especially good for the historical treatment of the minor doctrines of Jehovah's Witnesses. Its tone, however, is often harsh.

Van Buskirk, Michael. *The Scholastic Dishonesty of the Watchtower* (Santa Ana, California: Christian Apologetics: Research and Information Service, 1976).

This is an excellent, short 44-page treatment of the Jehovah's Witnesses misuse of Greek and Hebrew scholarship. It is thorough, completely documented, and the best single source to show the Jehovah's Witnesses that the Watchtower Society has misrepresented and misused Greek and Hebrew grammar in trying to support their own position.

Williams, J. L. *Victor Paul Wierville and The Way International* (Chicago, Illinois: Moody Press, 1979).

This is definitely the best work on the cult The Way International from a Christian perspective. An expert in the field, Williams deals with it doctrinally and historically.

Yamamoto, J. Isamu. *The Puppet Master: An Inquiry into Sun Myung Moon and the Unification Church* (Downers Grove, Illinois: InterVarsity Press, 1977).

Yamamoto is one of the leading Christian experts on the Unification Church. This book is well documented and deals extensively with Moon's doctrines and teachings.

Have You Heard of the
Four Spiritual Laws?

Just as there are physical laws that govern the physical universe, so are there spiritual laws which govern your relationship with God.

LAW ONE

GOD **LOVES** YOU, AND OFFERS A WONDERFUL **PLAN** FOR YOUR LIFE.

(References contained in this booklet should be read in context from the Bible wherever possible.)

Written by Bill Bright. Copyright © Campus Crusade for Christ, Inc., 1965. All rights reserved.

God's Love

"For God so loved the world, that He gave His only begotten Son, that whoever believes in Him should not perish, but have eternal life" (John 3:16).

God's Plan

(Christ speaking) "I came that they might have life, and might have it abundantly" (that it might be full and meaningful) (John 10:10).

Why is it that most people are not experiencing the abundant life? Because . . .

2 LAW TWO

MAN IS SINFUL AND SEPARATED FROM GOD. THEREFORE, HE CANNOT KNOW AND EXPERIENCE GOD'S LOVE AND PLAN FOR HIS LIFE.

Man Is Sinful

"For all have sinned and fall short of the glory of God" (Romans 3:23).

Man was created to have fellowship with God; but, because of his stubborn self-will, he chose to go his own independent way and fellowship with God was broken. This self-will, characterized by an attitude of active rebellion or passive indifference, is evidence of what the Bible calls sin.

Man Is Separated

"For the wages of sin is death" (spiritual separation from God) (Romans 6:23).

This diagram illustrates that God is holy and man is sinful. A great gulf separates the two. The arrows illustrate that man is continually trying to reach God and the abundant life through his own efforts, such as a good life, philosophy or religion.

The third law explains the only way to bridge this gulf . . .

---

3 LAW THREE

JESUS CHRIST IS GOD'S ONLY PROVISION FOR MAN'S SIN. THROUGH HIM YOU CAN KNOW AND EXPERIENCE GOD'S LOVE AND PLAN FOR YOUR LIFE.

He Died in Our Place

"But God demonstrates His own love toward us, in that while we were yet sinners, Christ died for us" (Romans 5:8).

He Rose from the Dead

"Christ died for our sins . . . He was buried . . . He was raised on the third day, according to the Scriptures . . . He appeared to Peter, then to the twelve. After that He appeared to more than five hundred . . ." (I Corinthians 15:3-6).

He Is the Only Way to God

"Jesus said to him, 'I am the way, and the truth, and the life; no one comes to the Father, but through Me' " (John 14:6).

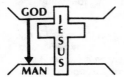

This diagram illustrates that God has bridged the gulf which separates us from Him by sending His Son, Jesus Christ, to die on the cross in our place to pay the penalty for our sins.

It is not enough just to know these three laws . . .

LAW FOUR

4

WE MUST INDIVIDUALLY **RECEIVE** JESUS CHRIST AS SAVIOR AND LORD; THEN WE CAN KNOW AND EXPERIENCE GOD'S LOVE AND PLAN FOR OUR LIVES.

We Must Receive Christ

"But as many as received Him, to them He gave the right to become children of God, even to those who believe in His name" (John 1:12).

We Receive Christ Through Faith

"For by grace you have been saved through faith; and that not of yourselves, it is the gift of God; not as a result of works, that no one should boast" (Ephesians 2:8,9).

When We Receive Christ, We Experience a New Birth.
(Read John 3:1-8.)

We Receive Christ by Personal Invitation

(Christ is speaking): "Behold, I stand at the door and knock; if any one hears My voice and opens the door, I will come in to him" (Revelation 3:20).

Receiving Christ involves turning to God from self (repentance) and trusting Christ to come into our lives to forgive our sins and to make us the kind of people He wants us to be. Just to agree intellectually that Jesus Christ is the Son of God and that He died on the cross for our sins is not enough. Nor is it enough to have an emotional experience. We receive Jesus Christ by faith, as an act of the will.

These two circles represent two kinds of lives:

SELF-DIRECTED LIFE
S — Self is on the throne
† — Christ is outside the life
• — Interests are directed by self, often resulting in discord and frustration

CHRIST-DIRECTED LIFE
† — Christ is in the life and on the throne
S — Self is yielding to Christ
• — Interests are directed by Christ, resulting in harmony with God's plan

Which circle best represents your life?
Which circle would you like to have represent your life?

The following explains how you can receive Christ:

YOU CAN RECEIVE CHRIST RIGHT NOW BY FAITH THROUGH PRAYER

(Prayer is talking with God)

God knows your heart and is not so concerned with your words as He is with the attitude of your heart. The following is a suggested prayer:

"Lord Jesus, I need You. Thank You for dying on the cross for my sins. I open the door of my life and receive You as my Savior and Lord. Thank You for forgiving my sins and giving me eternal life. Take control of the throne of my life. Make me the kind of person You want me to be."

Does this prayer express the desire of your heart?

If it does, pray this prayer right now, and Christ will come into your life, as He promised.

How to Know That Christ Is in Your Life

Did you receive Christ into your life? According to His promise in Revelation 3:20, where is Christ right now in relation to you? Christ said that He would come into your life. Would He mislead you? On what authority do you know that God has answered your prayer? (The trustworthiness of God Himself and His Word.)

The Bible Promises Eternal Life to All Who Receive Christ

"And the witness is this, that God has given us eternal life, and this life is in His Son. He who has the Son has the life; he who does not have the Son of God does not have the life. These things I have written to you who believe in the name of the Son of God, in order that you may know that you have eternal life" (I John 5:11-13).

Thank God often that Christ is in your life and that He will never leave you (Hebrews 13:5). You can know on the basis of His promise that Christ lives in you and that you have eternal life, from the very moment you invite Him in. He will not deceive you.

An important reminder . . .

DO NOT DEPEND UPON FEELINGS

The promise of God's Word, the Bible — not our feelings — is our authority. The Christian lives by faith (trust) in the trustworthiness of God Himself and His Word. This train diagram illustrates the relationship between **fact** (God and His Word), **faith** (our trust in God and His Word), and **feeling** (the result of our faith and obedience) (John 14:21).

The train will run with or without the caboose. However, it would be useless to attempt to pull the train by the caboose. In the same way, we, as Christians, do not depend on feelings or emotions, but we place our faith (trust) in the trustworthiness of God and the promises of His Word.

NOW THAT YOU HAVE RECEIVED CHRIST

The moment that you received Christ by faith, as an act of the will, many things happened, including the following:

1. Christ came into your life (Revelation 3:20 and Colossians 1:27).
2. Your sins were forgiven (Colossians 1:14).
3. You became a child of God (John 1:12).
4. You received eternal life (John 5:24).
5. You began the great adventure for which God created you (John 10:10; II Corinthians 5:17 and I Thessalonians 5:18).

Can you think of anything more wonderful that could happen to you than receiving Christ? Would you like to thank God in prayer right now for what He has done for you? By thanking God, you demonstrate your faith.

To enjoy your new life to the fullest . . .

SUGGESTIONS FOR CHRISTIAN GROWTH

Spiritual growth results from trusting Jesus Christ. "The righteous man shall live by faith" (Galatians 3:11). A life of faith will enable you to trust God increasingly with every detail of your life, and to practice the following:

G Go to God in prayer daily (John 15:7).

R Read God's Word daily (Acts 17:11)—begin with the Gospel of John.

O Obey God moment by moment (John 14:21).

W Witness for Christ by your life and words (Matthew 4:19; John 15:8).

T Trust God for every detail of your life (I Peter 5:7).

H Holy Spirit—allow Him to control and empower your daily life and witness (Galatians 5:16,17; Acts 1:8).

FELLOWSHIP IN A GOOD CHURCH

God's Word admonishes us not to forsake "the assembling of ourselves together. . ." (Hebrews 10:25). Several logs burn brightly together; but put one aside on the cold hearth and the fire goes out. So it is with your relationship to other Christians. If you do not belong to a church, do not wait to be invited. Take the initiative; call the pastor of a nearby church where Christ is honored and His Word is preached. Start this week, and make plans to attend regularly.

SPECIAL MATERIALS ARE AVAILABLE FOR CHRISTIAN GROWTH.

If you have come to know Christ personally through this presentation of the gospel, write for a free booklet especially written to assist you in your Christian growth.

A special Bible study series and an abundance of other helpful materials for Christian growth are also available. For additional information, please write Campus Crusade for Christ International, San Bernardino, CA 92414.

You will want to share this important discovery . . .